James Oram

Hogan

The story of a son of Oz

COLUMBUS BOOKS

LONDON

About the Author

James Oram and Paul Hogan got off to an unfortunate start. Not long after Hogan began his show-business career, Oram wrote a television column headed: 'Get This Ugly Australian Off TV.' An offended Hogan had to be persuaded that such criticism was a part of show business and that he shouldn't go to Oram's office and knock his block off. Oram has since then written extensively about Hogan and apparently been forgiven.

Oram has worked in newspapers and magazines in London and Sydney. He is now a special writer and columnist for the News Ltd group of newspapers in Sydney, has covered a dozen royal tours, three papal tours, and major stories in Australia, the South Pacific and South East Asia, including the guerilla war in the southern Philippines, the destruction of Darwin by Cyclone Tracy, the rebellion in Vanuatu, the heroin trade in Thailand, the Los Angeles Games and the America's Cup in Perth. A recent assignment, which came halfway through writing this book, was the army coup in Fiji.

For my father, Bert Oram,
for all he has done

Copyright © 1987 James Oram

First published in Great Britain in 1987 by
Columbus Books Limited
19-23 Ludgate Hill, London EC4M 7PD
Reprinted 1988

Designed by Fred Price
Chapter numerals by Mike Gordon

British Library Cataloguing in Publication Data
Oram, James
    Hogan: the story of a son of Oz.
    1. Hogan, Paul 2. Moving-picture actors
    and actresses—Australia—Biography
    I. Title
    791.43'028'0924   PN3018.H6/

    ISBN 0-86287-369-X

Phototypeset by Falcon Graphic Art Ltd
Wallington, Surrey
Printed in Hong Kong by Imago Publishing Ltd

Other books by James Oram

The People's Pope
The Business of Pop
The Hellraisers (*with Jim Fagin*)

Contents

1

Eagle on the brain

7

2

A looksee at the lingo

17

3

Larrikins at large

39

4

From Lightning Ridge to the
Harbour Bridge

49

5

A new face emerges

59

6

Just being himself

69

7

Commercial ventures

83

8

A drop of the amber nectar

97

9

An extra shrimp on the barbie

132

10

Crocodile tales

151

11

The outback meets the Big Apple

163

12

Assessing a super-whammo

177

13

And for his next trick?

187

Acknowledgements and bibliography

192

'I reckon God must have nodded off for a bit.'
Paul Hogan

On an ordinary June morning in an ordinary Sydney suburb, an extraordinary event occurred in the life and times of Paul Hogan. He was exercising his muscles at a gymnasium when an eagle swooped out of nowhere and buried its talons in his head. Just like that. No beg your bloody pardons. One moment he was lifting weights, the next his head was a ball of pain as the eagle clawed him. Hogan found this surprising. He knew Australia had three species of eagles, the wedge-tail, the sea eagle and the little eagle. The wedge-tail lived in timbered country and soared above the plains, preferring wallabies, possums and snakes to people's heads; the sea eagle's habitat was coastal and the little eagle remained in forests. As far as he was aware, eagles did not frequent the sweaty atmosphere of suburban indoor gymnasiums not far from the centre of Sydney, even if the particular gymnasium was in a suburb with the vaguely ornithological name of Crows Nest.

He swore. The pain got worse. His head was bursting.

When he left his home that morning and drove his Porsche 928S to the gymnasium, everything had seemed fine. He was feeling good. The family was happy. The bank account was swelling satisfactorily. And there were no problems with birds, let alone birds the size of eagles, for chrissake. The only birds ever to bother him were a few show-business vultures and the odd media galah.

The eagle struck in June, 1986, while he was bench-pressing 100 kilograms, not a big weight for a man who had kept himself superbly fit, especially when filming 'Crocodile' Dundee. On location he had worked out daily. The movie was now in the cinemas, where it was the biggest success in the history of the Australian box office. Soon it was to be released in the United States. '

Now this: a bloody great eagle! Its talons dug deeper and it crossed Hogan's mind that there was a fair chance he would die.

'I remember thinking the timing is ridiculous,' he later told Lenore Nicklin of *The Bulletin*.

I was as fit and healthy and happy as at any stage in my life. I thought it would be a pity to go at that stage. I didn't think, 'Oh, God, I didn't do that, I haven't seen China. I should've been nicer to so-and-so.'

I must have a pretty clear conscience. People ask if I rethought my priorities after an experience like that, but it was wasted on me. Usually people have those sort of experiences and rush off to work hard for charity or to climb Mount Everest. I think the only thing that hit me was I thought if I did die I'd had a good life and I wouldn't change a thing. And it reassured me that I am not worried about dying.

With the eagle still clutching his head, Hogan drove his car to Royal North Shore Hospital, a large complex close by, and presented himself at casualty. He was wheeled immediately into a cubicle for medical inspection.

'And who do we have here, sister?'

'Paul Hogan, doctor.'

'*The* Paul Hogan?'

'The very same.'

'What appears to be his problem?'

'He has an eagle sitting on his head.'

'An eagle? That's odd, shouldn't it be a crocodile?'

An examination revealed no trace of an eagle, not even where one had been. Rather, Hogan appeared to have suffered a cerebral haemorrhage. That was a relief! A cerebral haemorrhage was no publicans' picnic but it was an improvement on an eagle attached to the scone.

Actually, the notion of an eagle came later from Hogan, who enjoys a picturesque turn of phrase. It was one of his trademarks. It was expected.

'How did it feel?' a reporter asked Hogan on his release from hospital.

'Like an eagle came down out of the sky and fastened its talons into your head. All you can do is throw up and fight to stay conscious.'

Placed in a darkened room, Hogan was forbidden to do anything but blink – not that he was capable of much more, so intense was the pain. If he was worried, so was the Royal North Shore Hospital as it dawned upon administrative staff that they had under their care the most popular person in Australia, and at any moment the reptiles of the press, as William Cobbett so succinctly described them in 1823, would be slithering through the door. Every section of the media – television, radio, newspapers, weekly magazines, monthly magazines, obscure publications no one read – they'd all be there. The hospital did not make an official statement on the first day but with 700 patients, several hundred visitors and 4,000 staff, Hogan's admission wasn't going to remain the secret of Fatima. In fact, a couple of reptiles found out fairly soon and items were broadcast that night on television and radio.

The next morning Cindy Bradley, a public relations officer for the hospital, was called at six o'clock at her home and told that she better get to work fast because the media had gathered in strength.

'It took me by surprise,' she said. 'I knew he was popular but I didn't know he was *that* popular.' After dealing with the local media, she had to take calls from around the world. There would be no let-up for two weeks.

While Hogan lay in a darkened room on the seventh floor, the news that the nation's favourite son was as sick as a dog, which in Australia is very sick indeed, was the lead story on radio and television breakfast shows,

Hogan pictured with his wife Noelene. The couple married when Hogan was only nineteen.

the bulletins delivered in the grave, doom-laden tones usually reserved for prime ministers and pontiffs on the edge of eternity. The teak-tough 'Crocodile' Dundee was crook (ill) and all was not well with the nation. The two Sydney afternoon tabloid newspapers, the *Daily Mirror* and *The Sun*, leapt into action, despatching reporters and photographers to Hogan's home and to the hospital. Others were told to get on the telephone and ring anyone, relatives, friends, business associates, the milkman, for comments. This was big news. This was World War III. The *Daily Mirror* was on the streets at 9.30 a.m., its first three pages devoted to the story. Only the upper echelon of the royal family and Elizabeth Taylor got that much space.

At this stage it was generally accepted that Hogan had had a stroke, which to the lay person meant he would be partially paralysed. His family and friends played down the illness. Hogan's wife, Noelene, said: 'There's nothing drastic.' His manager, John Cornell, added: 'Don't worry about Hoges. He's not a tall poppy, he's an iron bark tree.' But people *were* worried. In the federal capital of Canberra, the Minister for Sport, Recreation and Tourism, John Brown, rose to his feet in the Australian Parliament and said: 'I am sure every member of this House, recognizing the enormous contribution Paul Hogan, the Australian of the Year, has made to the tourism industry, will join me in wishing his return to full health is very speedy.' For a few moments members of all political parties stopped verbally abusing each other in their sophisticated manner (which, over the years, had included such jolly insults as 'cowardly dirty hound', 'dumb dog', 'grinning jackanape', 'jabbering nincompoop', 'mongrel', 'pimp', 'scab', 'sewer rat', 'slimy reptile' and 'toad in a cesspit'). Donning their statesmen's masks, the members of the House of Representatives said, 'Hear, hear' to Brown's comments.

The Prime Minister, Robert James Lee Hawke, known to most Australians as Bob and to Hogan as Sparrow, sent a bunch of flowers, which some sections of the media thought a bit

Time for a cuppa? A young Hoges brews up an alternative version of the amber nectar.

poofy for 'Crocodile' Dundee. 'What else was he supposed to send?' sighed Hawke's press secretary, Paul Ellercamp. 'A crocodile?' The premier of New South Wales, Neville Wran, also aware that to ignore Hogan was political madness, expressed his shock and wished him well. The Mayor of Los Angeles, Tom Bradley, announced that Hogan's 'many friends in the United States, especially LA, wish him a speedy recovery.' Flowers and four thousand get-well cards and letters poured in from around the nation. Children sent small crocodiles made out of ring-pull tops. Only family and close friends were allowed to see him, but so many people turned up at the hospital that a security guard was employed to keep them away. 'Wish we had a security guard on the phones,' a harassed hospital switchboard operator muttered as the lights in front of her twinkled like Broadway.

So serious was the situation – at least as grave as losing a cricket test to England, the America's Cup to the United States or anything at all to France – that newspapers, as they do in times of crisis, were moved to editorialize. Said the *Daily Telegraph*:

Paul Hogan is a tall poppy. But unlike so many other successful men, nobody wants to chop him down. Apart from being a top entertainer and international movie star, he is also a top bloke. There was concern that the former knockabout Harbour Bridge rigger who has been a knockout as a top entertainer had been temporarily KO'd by a brain haemorrhage. Though he is still under observation, doctors have indicated that his condition is less serious than originally feared. Apart from the good wishes of his many friends and fans, Hogan received another well-deserved tonic yesterday with the news that his 'shrimp on the barbie' television commercials have been judged among the best in the United States. We join with all Australians in saying: Get well soon, Hoges.

The concern over Hogan's health was to be expected. Anyone who can make most of the population laugh has the stature of a national treasure and is treated as such. Hogan's illness was like dry rot in Westminster Abbey or mildew on the 'Mona Lisa'. Hogan was the mortal reminder that Australian humour was like no other – lean, sardonic, cynical, suspicious of authority, tempered by a harsh environment, honed by pessimism; it was gallows humour giving the two-finger salute to the hangman and saying 'Up yours for the rent, sport,' on the way to the scaffold. Someone suggested that Hogan personified Australian jokes that had been told and retold over the years, like this one.

A swagman, or tramp or hobo, was trudging along a bush road which, as is often the case, passed through huge paddocks, each one with a gate that had to be opened and closed so as not to let the cattle out. The day was scorching, there was no shade and the land was as flat as yesterday's beer.

Out of the distance came the cattle station owner in a cloud of dust and a big air-conditioned Cadillac. 'Jump in,' he said. 'I'll give you a lift.'

The swagman merely shook his head and kept walking.

Not wishing to see a fellow human suffer, the station owner pulled alongside the swagman once more. 'Don't be a bloody fool,' he said. 'Get in and I'll give you a ride.'

The swagman shook his head. 'No thanks, mate,' he said. 'You can open your own bloody gates.'

However, Paul Hogan, lying in Royal North Shore Hospital, was hardly in the mood or condition to assess Australian humour. He hurt too much. He was flat on his back, two needles every three hours, an intravenous drip in his arm, and was feeling as miserable as an orphan bandicoot on a burnt ridge. He was also wondering why in hell he was in hospital when he should have had his feet up taking it easy before embarking on a planned American promotional tour for 'Crocodile' Dundee . . . or counting his money. After all, he wasn't a sickly person. He was in extremely good health and after being examined for insurance policies for the film had three medical certificates to prove it. His blood pressure was fine. He had never had a headache. But here he was unable to move in a room surrounded by so many flowers it could have been a Mafia funeral.

'Do you need a bigger room?' he was asked one day.

'What for? It's got a bed, walls. What more do I need?'

Unable to read or watch television, he took to hallucinating. He quite enjoyed what he saw. 'I didn't want to miss anything. I was wriggling toes and fingers and counting up to ten to see if the brain was still functioning. That's why I hallucinated so much. I sort of enjoyed the hallucinations. I looked forward to them – they broke the monotony.'

In between hallucinating, he thought a bit about life and death, chatting to his alter-ego Hoges, the extrovert character clad in football shorts, sleeveless shirt and boots he had introduced to Australian television audiences twelve years earlier. 'I wanted to have a brush with death, but Hoges wouldn't let me. I kept thinking, "That's it, I'm going to die and that's a pity." But Hoges was running around saying, "Well, you might be going but I'm not. Bugger you!" It was a mistake. God must have nodded off and woke up and said, "What are they doing to Hoges?" and fixed it.'

'Were you really concerned?' Lee Dillow, Hogan's personal assistant on 'Crocodile' Dundee, asked later.

'I was a bit worried but Hoges didn't give a shit.'

The days passed. Hogan was poked and probed by doctors who concluded that his brain haemorrhage was a mild one, which came as a relief.

I'm one of the luckiest people alive. While I was in here a 27-year-old girl came in with a cerebral haemorrhage and she's now a paraplegic. Only eight per cent of people who have a cerebral haemorrhage have ones that do no damage, require no surgery, have no lasting effects and never recur. I was lucky. I had one like that: it burst in a part of the brain that's never used and it did no damage and it wasn't life-threatening.

He may also have recalled a time two years before when he thought he had suffered a stroke. It occurred in London after filming a commercial for Foster's lager. His reaction to dying was much the same as when he had a cerebral haemorrhage. Several months after the haemorrhage he told the story to Phil Jarratt of Australian *Playboy*:

'Vote for Hoges' was a 1980 TV sketch – but his 1986 illness was noticed by the Australian House of Representatives.

There was a party for the crew that night. Got full of ink and went to bed. Woke up a few hours later numb down my left side and my fingers tingling. I thought: stroke. I remember lyin' there in me hotel bed thinking, you can't complain, Hoges, you've had a good dig. I thought, well, the wife and kids are covered, the trust account'll take care of them. Travellers' cheques. I remembered I'd put them under the cupboard or somewhere and they mightn't find them when they found the body. There are a lot of things you gotta think about when you're dyin'. I got up to get the cheques and I was standing up okay. Then I looked in the mirror and saw this dirty big red line right down my face and body. What had happened was I'd collapsed into bed with me head and arm hangin' over the dressing table, cutting off me circulation. I was right again in a few minutes. I was bloody glad I didn't go and wake everyone up.

Daily bulletins kept a worried public up to date with his medical condition. Not since the noble racehorse Phar Lap died in 1932, with the then Prime Minister, Joe Lyons, leading the mourning, had there been so much concern over one national figure, proving once more that Australian priorities differ from those of other countries. Britain might get emotional over the health of a great actor, America a president, France an artist, Japan an automobile manufacturer – but Australia reserved its anxiety for a middle-aged comedian who helped sell two products supposedly bad for the human system: cigarettes and beer. And in case the public wasn't getting enough information on Hogan's illness, newspapers brought in their own specialists to explain the complicated and fiddly bits. The *Sydney Morning Herald* observed:

The brain haemorrhage Paul Hogan suffered, if more severe, could have caused a stroke and possibly death, according to one doctor. A brain haemorrhage, or a cerebrovascular accident, occurs when a blood vessel in the brain spontaneously bursts, causing internal bleeding. While the condition is different from an actual blockage of a blood vessel, both can result in a stroke. A vessel may burst for one or two primary reasons. First, as a result of high blood pressure or because of a condition called berry aneurysm, which causes weak spots in the blood vessels. Vessels may also burst as the result of a blow to the skull. A brain haemorrhage may cause damage by exerting pressure on sections of the brain and by starving areas of

the brain of vital blood supply containing oxygen and vital nutrients because of loss of blood from the system. A stroke can be caused by either complication.

Hogan was indeed lucky, more so if he managed to avoid reading complicated medical analyses in newspapers.

After two weeks Hogan went home. After losing 4.5 kilograms (about 10 lbs) he was so weak he couldn't have knocked the skin off a rice pudding. 'We want to fatten him up,' said Noelene Hogan, serving him a meal of steak and eggs, the Australian national dish in spite of the efforts of restaurant owners to popularize *cuisine minceur*.

Hogan's manager, John Cornell, announced there would be a media conference when Hogan was strong enough, but Brett Thomas, of the Sydney *Sun*, beat his rivals by calling on Hogan at his Belrose home. He had tried before but Noelene Hogan had come to the door and shaken her head. With photographer John O'Grady, Thomas was in the area and reckoned another attempt wouldn't go astray. Crunching down the long gravel driveway past a vast sweep of lawn, he knocked on the front door. Hogan appeared, unshaven and dressed in old jeans and a blue sweater, accompanied by his dog.

'How're you going, Hoges?' he asked.

'I'm terrific,' said Hogan. 'I wouldn't be dead for quids [money].'

He denied stress had anything to do with the cerebral haemorrhage, and, remembering he was in show business, reminded the public that 'Crocodile' Dundee was still in the cinemas and that those who hadn't seen it were close to being unpatriotic. 'I read in some newspapers they blamed stress and overwork for what happened, but that's all crap. It had nothing to do with it. The hardest decision I ever had to make was whether to go out and mow the backyard or not. And look at the success of 'Crocodile' Dundee – it's the biggest-grossing entertainment event in this country of all time. It's outsold *ET*, it's outsold the Moscow Circus and it's even outsold Dire Straits. What have I got to be stressed about?'

A couple of days before his wife had said much the same thing. 'I've never known Paul to be stressed at all. He's always totally in command. People were saying he was run-down and tired – he never gets tired. Probably the only time he's been stressed was on our wedding day.'

Soon afterwards Hogan held his media conference. In cream cricket sweater, cream trousers, pale slubbed cotton jacket and tan stockman boots, he looked as flash as a rat with a gold tooth as he walked into the packed room, preceded by John Cornell, who announced with the flourish of a town-crier or a papal attendant: 'Paul Hogan . . . by special arrangement with God.'

'G' day, viewers,' Hogan said, as flashlights flared and microphones were stuck up his nose. Tanned from a brief holiday in Fiji, he looked well enough.

'How're you going, Hoges?' the media asked as one. Hogan said how he was going and how he had been, then demonstrated that his sojourn in hospital was history by getting

Hogan has publicly stated that he wouldn't run for prime minister of Australia, because he'd 'probably get the job'. The man holding the placard is Michael Willesee, the Australian news programme presenter.

stuck into politicians, even those who had sent flowers and said nice things. In fact, his political thoughts occupied more of the conference than did his trumpet-blowing on behalf of 'Crocodile' Dundee:

Politicians don't know what's wrong with this country – and if they do, they don't know how to fix it. Y'know, Australia needs a lot of things to be put right and I reckon I could do that. But I can't see myself being a Prime Minister if I have to become a politician. Politicians always get caught up with party politics and they are all dunces, anyway. There're only about two things politicians think about when they're elected to power: that's how to get re-elected and how to raise taxes so that they can afford to get back in office. To run the country, I'd have to be a benevolent dictator. Prime Minister Hawke doesn't run this country. Nobody does. I won't become Prime Minister because if I did I would be ineffective and that's not the idea. As an entertainer I'm more effective than a politician because people watch and listen to me. No entertainer should use fame to get behind a wagon and push a cause. I have my views on life and I've done my bit for Australia with tourism. I don't need to do any more because Australia is not a bloody charity. Australians should get off their backsides and help themselves.

Hogan had put his nose into the political arena before, but only as a comedian in spite of the efforts of political parties to commandeer his appeal. In 1974 he was offered what was said to be a considerable amount of money to lend his support to the Liberal Party (conservative) of Western Australia by way of television commercials and public appearances. Australian political parties have long held the belief that show-business personalities, no matter what their experience, can be successful in politics, and, of course, Ronald Reagan proved them right. Hogan knocked back the Western Australian offer by saying: 'I would never try to influence people in their political views.' But now he was advocating a political dictatorship. It may have been Hoges speaking and not Hogan, though sometimes it was difficult to tell the difference. Hoges lived down the street from Hogan but they sometimes got together to speak with the one voice.

That he would have won any political contest was never doubted. Before the 1980 general election he had performed a skit, 'Hoges for PM', and 70,000 people had written his name on their polling papers. In 1983, a year of gloomy political predictions, of sleeves up and noses to the grindstone, he had again given his, or Hoges', views:

My policies would be radical. Bring back beheading. That sort of stuff. I'll show some imagination, not like the two blokes we've got at the moment. They've promised us nothing but disappointment and gloom. I liked the old-fashioned politicians, the good old days when we got promised all sorts of heavens: no tax; things will be prosperous; everyone will have jobs. We knew they couldn't keep the promises and we didn't hold them to it but it was cheerful.

In 1986, however, things were serious; even the unions were becoming aware that all was not well in what had been called 'the lucky country'. Hogan was delivering what the public wanted. And furthermore politicians are generally regarded by Australians as being slightly lower than a snake's belly, a statement with which Honourable Members have sometimes agreed. The Federal Minister for Tourism, John Brown, once commented: 'Politicians are only two notches above child-molesters on the social scale.'

Hogan later expanded on his views of Prime Minister Hawke and a political dictatorship. He said that although he was not interested in going into politics he was arrogant enough to think he could run the country.

My gut feeling on the day was that Bob Hawke had slipped. I thought he was the great white hope. He isn't. Unfortunately, I've suddenly become a radio pundit. Radio stations want me to talk about the Prime Minister and the government and what they should be doing. My job is to make people forget them . . . Part of what I said was tongue-in-cheek but, no doubt about it, the country does need shakin' up. Someone like me has a habit of saying something that reflects a general gut feeling throughout the country. If I'm sayin' it, then all the pub spokesmen around the country are sayin' it too.

All the same, he did not let up on his idea of a benevolent dictatorship. Several months later he told the British magazine *Time Out*, a publication for Hampstead Heath socialists, that Australia needed such a dictatorship:

You can only afford the luxuries of the left wing – save the whales, stop uranium mining, grants to the arts, increasing pensions – if you are a prosperous right-wing country. A dictator should step in and abolish the left-wing and handouts. Then, after four or five years, the country'll be back on the rails and we can bring back all the benevolent left-wing services.

He added that the British Prime Minister, Margaret Thatcher, did not 'come on strong enough'. Hogan has never declared which political party he supports but the casual observer would conclude that it can't be the Trotskyites.

The Sydney *Sun* immediately asked several politicians, including Federal Liberal member Michael Hodgman, why Hogan would be good for Australia.

'Paul is taller than Bob Hawke,' said Hodgman. 'I'd like to see a tall Prime Minister. I'm sick of this short one.'

The newspaper then ran a competition inviting readers to write in suggesting how Hogan should run the country, the first prize being a seven-day holiday in the Northern Territory where 'Crocodile' Dundee was filmed.

The court jester was back with his cap and bells and all was well with the country.

After interviewing Paul Hogan in London in 1984, a British journalist, John Patrick, wrote: 'Even in the £800-a-week rented house he and "his mates" have been staying in, he played his Aussie character to the hilt. Entering the chandeliered dining room he sprawled on one of the elegant chairs, put his boots up on the polished mahogany table and enquired if we [the photographer and myself] would care to join him in a "sanger".

' "Pardon?"

' "A sanger," he intoned in the loud, slow voice one uses when addressing an elderly, deaf relative. He held up what appeared to be two halves of a loaf of bread connected precariously in the middle by a filling of lettuce, cold meat, gherkins, with tomatoes dripping out of the sides.

' "Ah, a sandwich," I ventured.

'Hogan raised an eyebrow, stared straight through me, wiped his hand across his partly filled mouth and asked threateningly: "You takin' the mick, mate?"

' "No, no, not at all, Mr Hogan," I said, sipping quickly at my beer . . .

'I gingerly speculated that his boots, T-shirt, shorts and uncouth manner may be just

an act and underneath a more serious Hogan lay unconcealed.

' "Nah. Oh, I admit I bung it on a bit for you press drongoes but Hoges on the telly and me off have a lot in common. Neither of us gives a bugger what people think. Well, I don't have to, do I?"

'But surely he doesn't dress like this all the time? "Don't be one all yer life, son. Of course yer don't. Only when yer home. No, when yer out on the street yer dress like everyone else. When in Rome do as the Poms do."

'And England? "Well, yer don't have to be funny here, do yer? The whole place is a joke. When I tell 'em at home you've got a sheila as prime minister they go hysterical. Besides, any outfit that reckons it's normal to have warm beer, cold pies and little rocks on the beaches instead of sand has got to be funny. Still, I've met a lot of interesting people."

'A girl came in and said she had almost finished packing for their flight home that afternoon.

' "Yer blood's worth bottlin', love. I'll finish up. Be good to get home, but. Had a real grouse time here. And the neighbours around here were all right – well, except for the flag. See, the Jordanian Embassy or something's next door. And, you know, they're always blueing [fighting among themselves]. So just in case any bomb-thrower got his addresses mucked up, I threw out an Aussie flag from the balcony. But the coppers made me take it down. Said the local residents were upset.

' "Funny about London this time, but. I was 'ere ten years ago. Now there don't seem to be many Poms left. Well, got to finish packin'. I'm missin' the missus and the billy lids [kids]. Ooroo [Goodbye]."

'Outside I said to the photographer: "He's as game as Ned Kelly. A real grouse bloke. Come on, I'll shout you a drop of the amber nectar in the pub."

'He stopped, looked at me and said: "It must be wonderful to be bilingual." '

The journalist had made a brave attempt to come to terms with Australian slang, the language of Paul Hogan and the average bloke in

'She'll be right, mate': an Aussie gesture that surmounts all linguistic barriers.

the pub. It is a colourful, growing language that in its broadest can sound like a foreign tongue to someone from, say, Manchester, United Kingdom, or Manchester, United States. Until Hogan came on the scene, Australians were often embarrassed by the way they talked; it was another chip on the shoulder. As Hogan put it:

There's no doubt that most Australians suffer from a national inferiority complex. And until recently, all our TV people aped either a British or an American accent – anything not to speak with a true native accent because it was considered low-class. They were speakin' this ridiculous Oxford English accent that they don't even speak in England. The other half were copying a kind of California-American accent. I was talkin' like the guys down at the pub. Like an Australian. Simple – but believe it or not, everyone thought it was bloody amazing.

John Bernard, Professor of Linguistics at Macquarie University (Sydney),who is on the advisory Committee to the Australian Broadcasting Commission and on the editorial committee of the *Macquarie Dictionary*, agreed with Hogan that Australians cringed at the sound of their accents. He said in 1986 that many Australians, believing they were cultured and eloquent, tried to sound like the English upper-classes but instead simply sounded wrong:

The first white Australians, the convicts, were uneducated, unclean and probably illegitimate. Australia was a frontier society and nothing was important except having a meal on the table. By 1850, when there was some pattern of education, school inspectors were horrified by the local speech and called for a 'halt to this vicious dialect'.

Another stout defender of the accent was Dr John Ingram, lecturer in English at Queensland University, who said: 'The broad Australian accent is a legitimate form of speech and should not be stigmatized as a speech defect needing correction.'

Ron Saw, in *The Bulletin* magazine (1982), put forward an amusing, if unlikely, theory for Australian speech. He said the fault lay with English lawyers who insisted on using long-dead Latin:

The average Oz, when asked if he agreed that *Rex peccare non potet* – vaguely, the king can do no wrong – put out his tongue and made a rude noise which became known later as the Australian language. The Greek migrants refused to have anything to do with Latin, while the Turks, Arabs and Indians, who already made rude noises of their own, swelled the babble and – lo and behold! – around our very ears grew an entirely new language: one which should now be used by those of us to whom English remains a mystery.

The Australian accent is not mellifluous. Honey does not drop from each word. The accent moved American actor Robert Easton to say in 1979: 'I've heard John Newcombe describe a tennis match, and if I came close to imitating that I believe I could impersonate a wild duck singing "Annie Laurie" underwater.' Humorist Buzz Kennedy agreed in his column in the newspaper The Australian: 'The broad Australian accent is not a lovesome thing, I grant you. At its worst, it is reminiscent of a dehydrated crow uttering its last statement on life from the bough of a dead tree in the middle of a claypan at the peak of a seven-year drought.'

According to popular belief, the reason why the Australian accent can be offensive to the ear is flies. Australians speak as if there were a tax on lip movement because to open their mouths further would be to allow in flies. Australia has 6,800 species of flies and every single one seems anxious to inspect the dental work of anyone who opens his mouth beyond a slit, not only in the bush but sometimes in the centre of such large cities as Sydney. Ever willing to rinse the colour from life, academics dismiss the fly theory, suggesting instead that laziness is the reason. Sir Herman Black, Chancellor of the University of Sydney, said in 1982: 'Australians swallow more syllables than any other single line of consumption.'

But the distinguished Australian thespian Walter Sullivan has also blamed it on the flies. Able to drop a well-rounded line of Shakespeare with the best of them, he says he has been forced to change his delivery when speaking in rural areas. 'On those occasions, mostly in West Australian and Queensland country areas, I found it difficult to speak in rounded tones because one's mouth had to be kept partially closed to keep out the bushflies.'

Another explanation is offered by Bill Hor-nadge, who has spent a lifetime observing the idiosyncrasies of Australians. He believes the harsh environment is to blame. In his work The Australian Slanguage (1986) he said that the heat of the continent was hard on the early settlers, most of whom came from much colder climates in the Northern Hemisphere. They quickly discovered they had no energy to waste; therefore:

It would be a perfectly logical defence mechanism for the organs of speech to slow down their tempo in line with the natural slowing of other body rhythms. The opening of the mouth to enunciate clearly is wasteful of energy, whereas clipped and abbreviated speech uttered through lips that open fractionally reduces jaw action and conserves energy. If we are a nation of mumblers, there may be perfectly sound evolutionary reasons why this is so. I am well aware that such a theory is probably as incapable of scientific proof as the fly theory; but at least it is worth advancing as a possible explanation of our curious speech patterns.

Since time immemorial, Australians have found it easier to abbreviate the language, to hack sentences in half and shave letters from words, the time saved being spent on more rewarding pursuits such as drinking beer and studying race form. The author Robert Treborlang, in How to Survive in Australia (1985), gives an example of Australian conversation:

'Not bad, eh?'
'Could've been worse.'
'My oath!'
'Makes you think.'
'You're not wrong there.'
'Might change, but.'
'Pretty unlikely.'
'You never know.'
'Fair enough.'

This conversation would be understood perfectly by the average Australian but would be lost on British and Americans. They would be further confused if they listened to a person abbreviating words, which many do most of the time; for example:

Thommo [Thompson] had a cuppa [cup of tea] for brekkie [breakfast], listening to the trannie [tran-

Cultured, eloquent – the average ocker also believes in keeping himself super-fit by indulging in a range of sports.

sistor radio] for the results of last night's footy [football] and trots [trotting races], where he'd bet on a few roughies [long shots]. But the bookie [bookmaker] had won again. He wondered if he should take a sickie [sick leave] because he wanted to sink a few tinnies [beer cans] in the arvo [afternoon], especially since his wife was in Brissie [Brisbane] on hols [holiday]. Or maybe he could go to the beach, except he needed a new cozzie [swimming costume]. The postie [postman] arrived with a letter from his sister in Tassie [Tasmania] saying she was preggers [pregnant]. Deciding to go to work, he got into his ute [utility truck], although the carby [carburettor] gave him problems, and noted that the rego [motor registration] was due. Later in Paddo [Paddington] he met his mates Davo [Davidson] and Hendo [Henderson], then went to the deli [delicatessen] for food and insect spray for the mossies [mosquitoes] and blowies [blowflies]. 'This shortening of the lingo [language] is causing me aggro [aggravation],' he said to himself as he slipped into his jarmies [pyjamas] and bed.

Critics of Australian speech, or knockers (not to be confused with female breasts) as they're called, have dismissed the abbreviation of words as childish, proof that Australia has not grown up. It should be noted that the criticism usually comes from Britain and grows in proportion to the number of English wickets taken by Australian bowlers or to the size of Australia's winning margin in rugby union tests.

Even in the early days of settlement Australians were determined to speak differently, preferably while drinking. In *Southern Lights and Shadows* (1859) F. Fowler observed:

In Sydney and its immediate neighbourhood, there are no less than 500 public houses, many of them as great and garish as the gin palaces of London . . . At present these drinking habits are ruining a large class of the population. Nothing is done without the nobbler. Merchants keep the bottle in their offices, and the first question put to you, even by respectable men, is, 'What are you going to drink?' In fact not to drink is considered a crime . . . Here, too – as in America – the bottle has its literature. To pay for liquor for another is to 'stand', or to 'shout', or to 'sacrifice'. The measure is called a 'nobbler', or a 'breakdown' . . .

There is little doubt that some of the Australian vernacular had its origins in Britain, or to

be more precise in London. This is the Cockney factor. Dr Rabbi Brasch of Sydney, who for nearly 30 years has been delving into the origins of words, agrees there is a definite Cockney influence. 'Probably the predominant Cockney, together with the Irish accent of our early settlers, gave us the mix which has made the Australian accent unique,' he said in 1985. 'I don't believe it has changed all that much over the past century. Post-war migrants have certainly forced us to add new words to our vocabulary – as has the influence of overseas film and television shows. But it hasn't changed our accent, and doesn't look likely to.'

The Cockney influence is seen at its strongest in the Australian use of rhyming slang. Australia is probably the only place in the world beyond the sound of Bow Bells where rhyming slang is still tossed into conversation like currants into a cake. Geoff McCamey wrote this sentence in the *Sunday Telegraph* (1984): 'Pull up a Cain and Fred and let's have a pickled about being a currant to the Jack.' He interpreted it thus: 'Pull up a table [Cain and Abel] and chair [Fred Astaire], and let's have a talk [pickled pork] about being awake [currant cake] to the slang [Jack Lang].' Jack Lang, incidentally, was a controversial Labour Premier of New South Wales who was dismissed in 1932 by the NSW Governor, Sir Phillip Game, an act for which some members of the Labour Party have never forgiven Britain.

But sometimes the passage from the slang to the actual meaning becomes so convoluted it is almost impossible to track down the connection. An example is L.K.S., which ultimately equates with water. The term derives from the L.K.S. Mackinnon Stakes, the lead-up race to the Melbourne Cup, a sporting event of such importance that the State of Victoria declares an official holiday to enable workers to go to the track to keep the bookmakers in Rolls-Royces and mansions. The L.K.S. Mackinnon Stakes is run over 2,000 metres, which is 10 furlongs, which is a mile and a quarter –

Hogan as the bush philosopher, spinning yarns round the campfire. Something of this early TV character went into the personality of 'Mick' (Michael J.) Dundee.

which, of course, rhymes with water. Simple.

The use of rhyming slang is probably on the wane, except in prisons, where it is widely used in the hope that the screws (warders) won't know what is being said, or plotted. As new generations grow up and do their time, the rhymes change; thus 'wank', which not only means to masturbate but also behaviour which is self-indulgent and egotistical, was once 'board and plank'; now it's 'Sherman tank'.

The greatest asset of Australian language is its colourful phrases, which some observers believe are in danger of being lost and replaced by Americanisms. The phrases are unique. For instance, 'Stone the crows!', an exclama-tion of astonishment, had to be removed from the movie 'Crocodile' Dundee for the American market. Paul Hogan has revealed that when the film was initially tested in the United States everyone looked at the sky after the exclamation was uttered, expecting to see a shower of stones hurtling towards a flock of crows.

The Adelaide critic Max Harris has observed that many Australian colloquialisms are in danger of obsolescence, mourning the passing of such expressions as 'off like a bride's nightie', 'flat out like a lizard drink-ing', and 'send her down, Hughie'. Harris has obviously spent too long in ivory towers, for these expressions are widely used in the pubs

Instant Guide to Australian Lingo

(non-Australians wishing to pass as sons or daughters of Oz are advised to learn these words and phrases off by heart)

Dry as a kookaburra's khyber [Khyber Pass, rhyming slang for arse] in the desert.
Shot through like a Bondi tram [moved quickly].
Happy as a possum up a gum tree.
Come the raw prawn [try to put some-thing over): 'Don't you come the raw prawn with me.'
Dressed up like a pox doctor's clerk [flashily dressed but not always in good taste].
There's no flies on him [he's smart].
Better than a poke in the eye with a burnt stick.
Like an old moll at a christening [out of place]: 'When Fred, the garbo [gar-bage man], went to Buckingham Palace he felt like an old moll at a christening.'

Miserable as a bastard on Father's Day.
Dry as a Pommy's towel.
A smile like a wave in a slop bucket.
Running around like a headless chook.
Doesn't know if he's Arthur or Martha [confused].
In like Flynn [after Australian actor Errol Flynn: to grab an opportunity, usually sexual].
She'd talk under wet cement.
Drinking with the flies [drinking alone].
Send her down, Hughie [a farmer's cry to the heavens when rain starts falling].
His blood's worth bottling [he is extreme-ly helpful].
A kangaroo loose in the top paddock [a crazy person].
As lonely as a shag on a rock.
He's a two-pot screamer [gets drunk quickly].
Sat there like a stunned mullet [dazed].
So windy it would blow a dog off the chain.
Don't get off your bike, I'll pick up the pump [soothing response to an angry person].
Crook [ill] as Rookwood [Rookwood Cemetery, Sydney].
The scrub was so thick a dog couldn't bark in it.

and clubs of the suburbs and rural areas. Only recently in an inner city pub I overheard a conversation which went something like this:

'I'm just about to put the hard work on her when her boyfriend arrives, so I'm off like a bride's nightie.'

'Good thing, mate. He does his lolly [loses his temper].'

'Yeah, he's as silly as a two-bob watch. And mean. He wouldn't shout [buy a drink] if a shark bit him.'

'Too right, he's got snakes in his pockets. Anyhow, how's the punting?'

'No luck, mate. If it was raining palaces I'd be hit by a dunny door.'

'Know what you mean. I've been up and down like a dunny seat at a mixed party.'

And so on. It was worth the price of a beer to hear them talking.

Perhaps the expression that for better or worse sums up the Australian character is 'she'll be right'. It reflects the happy-go-lucky attitude of Australians, who cheerfully reassure anyone that what is wrong will be fixed up sooner or later – preferably later. This infuriates Japanese and American businessmen who have invested heavily in Australia and pride themselves on efficiency. As Bill Hornadge puts it in *The Australian Slanguage*:

The trait is most evident in planning events or functions. The Australian is a willing enough work-

---

Wouldn't know him if he fell out of a packet of cornflakes.

Don't be one all your life [don't be silly].

Not worth two shakes of a lamb's tail [not worth much].

Couldn't fight his way out of a paper bag.

He couldn't work in an iron lung [a lazy person].

Wouldn't know his arse from a hole in the ground [to be ill informed].

Cop the blue [take the blame].

Give it a burl [make an attempt].

Hope your chooks turn to emus and kick your dunny down [untranslatable term of abuse].

Cooking with gas [being in control of a situation].

Fair crack of the whip [give a person a fair go].

Up shit creek without a paddle [in serious trouble].

Rattle your dags [hurry up].

Face as long as a month of Sundays [dismal expression].

Put in for the mob [fart in company without owning up to it].

Who's robbing this coach [mind your own business]?

Mad as a gumtree full of galahs [extremely stupid].

Run like a hairy goat [run slowly, usually a horse].

Have him by the short and curlies [have him in your control].

Hit the kick [pay up]: 'It's about your turn to hit the kick for a beer.'

All over the place like a madwoman's breakfast [disarray].

Fit as a mallee bull [extremely fit].

All piss and wind [insincere].

Wouldn't piss on him if he was on fire [wouldn't help].

Rare as hen's teeth [extremely rare].

Moved like a rat up a drainpipe [moved very quickly].

Rough as guts [very rough].

Shake hands with the wife's best friend [to urinate].

Things are crook in Tallarook [situation is not good].

Seen more tails than Hoffmann [referring to Offenbach's opera *Tales of Hoffmann*: applied to a racehorse that always runs well back in the field].

He couldn't give away cheese at a rat's picnic.

He couldn't get a screw in a brothel [not good at organizing things].

Know you? I'd know your skin if I saw it hanging on a bush.

er when he sees something has to be done, but he is a very poor planner and leaves all sorts of things to chance in a manner that gives ulcers to those who have to come along and pick up the bits and pieces.

It's probably the Irish in us, which is nowhere described better than in *Australia – What Is It?* (1971) by Henry Williams:

If the madmen triumph and the button is pressed and this earth is reduced to a smouldering radioactive cinder, maybe, out on the old Barcoo or somewhere out west, there will be a survivor, a lone battler to emerge from his timber-and-corrugated shack, look out across the ruined planet, roll himself a smoke, and say: 'She'll be right, mate.'

Paul Hogan scatters his conversation with such expressions. They come naturally from his days and nights in working-class areas, but one would have to be a dill to believe he doesn't work on them these days. It's like his homework. Those featured on pages 24-5 are a few he may use, or if he doesn't some other Australian will.

When it comes to insults, Australia is a gold-mine. There are words for every occasion, most of them splendidly offensive, and with the right inflection can result in an interesting stoush (brawl). Ned Kelly, the famous bushranger (bandit, highwayman), is remembered for two things. One was his spectacular gun battle at Glenrowan, Victoria, in 1890, which lasted twelve hours before Ned, clad in armour made from plough shares, was wounded and captured. The other was his famous letter to the authorities, in which he gave the Victorian police a character reading. 'A parcel of big, ugly, fat-necked, wombat-headed, big-bellied, magpie-legged, narrow-hipped, splay-footed sons of Irish bailiffs or English landlords which is better known as Officers of Justice or Victorian Police.'

Perhaps Australia's best gift to the world was the word 'wowser', a description applied to a member of that melancholy species opposed to such amiable pleasures as drinking, gambling, smoking, enjoying oneself on the Sabbath and looking at dirty pictures. The *Macquarie Dictionary* definition is 'a prudish teetotaller, a killjoy'. The American writer H.L. Mencken, who enjoyed the word so much he tried to introduce it into the American language, described a wowser as 'a drab-souled Philistine haunted by the mockery of others' happiness. Every Puritan is not necessarily a wowser; to be one he must devote himself zealously to reforming the morals of his neighbors, and, in particular, to throwing obstacles in the way of their enjoyment of what they choose to regard as pleasures.'

The origin of 'wowser' has been the subject of debate for years but it is generally accepted that Ezra Norton, the larrikin owner of the Sydney newspaper *Truth*, if he didn't actually invent the word, made it popular at the turn of the century. He defined it as 'a single, simple word that does at once describe, deride, and denounce that numerous, noxious, pestilent, puritanical kill-joy push – the whole blasphemous, wire-whiskered brood.' Norton said he was 'proud of my invention. The fabrication of such a word – absolutely absent from, but absolutely required in our local vernacular, until I invented it – was a stroke of genius, done on the spur of the moment, impromptu, the result of divine or diabolical inspiration . . . To my humble self – to me, John Norton, alone belongs the sole undivided glory and renown of inventing a single word . . .'

Another splendid word is 'bludger', which Australia stole from Britain and turned to its own use. The British meaning is a description of anyone living off the earnings of a prostitute. Australia leapt on the word with gusto and, as Max Harris pointed out: 'Only in Australia did the word (and what a savage and telling word it is) acquire the meaning of any sort of parasitical behaviour. In Britain they have "social welfare cheats". In Australia "dole bludgers"! What a difference in denigratory force!'

The problem with Australian slang, at least to the outsider, is that one word can mean many things. Take 'bastard', which means illegitimate. You can call a man, or even a woman, a bastard in Australia and receive a smack in the mouth for your troubles. But if you said, 'He's not a bad bastard', it would be taken as a compliment. Elizabeth Johnston, in *The Australian* (1981), related a story that told something about the word. The Queensland

The 'Hoges for PM' TV skit: would Hogan ever take on Bob Hawke?

Governor, Sir Lesley Wilson, went on an expedition in search of the delicious mudcrab with fisherman Snowy Maltman.

Everything went well for a while. The aide-de-camp was rowing smoothly and Snowy and his mate were sharing the light and the scoop duty with precision.

'The Governor asked if he could work the spotlight,' Snowy recalled. 'Well, the next time we spotted a crab he got excited and waved the light all over the place and I just turned around and said: "Here, give it to me, you stupid bastard."

'I apologized straight away but he said it was perfectly all right, he had been a stupid bastard.'

As Bill Hornadge says in *The Australian Slanguage*, the word is taken so seriously there is an organization called The Antedeluvian Order of Old Bastards, with chapters in all capital cities and in some country towns.

The irregular meetings of these chapters seem given over to much liquor consumption and considerable emphasis on stories in the vein of 'Bastards I met recently . . .' Members carry around in their wallets visiting cards proclaiming they are regular Old Bastards, and some even wear lapel badges advertising this strange piece of information – no doubt to the great astonishment of new arrivals in the country exposed for the first time to one of Australia's more unnerving and bizarre institutions.

'Crook' is another confusing word. It means, as it does world-wide, a criminal, but also a feeling of illness ('Jeez, I feel crook') or to tell someone off ('The missus went crook at me when I came home from the pub feeling crook').

Slang is so entrenched in Australia that churches, always on the lookout for new ways to attract customers, have translated the Bible into the Australian idiom. Some Bible stories were recorded on cassettes under the title *The*

Pope Hoges, in a Religious Olympics for the TV show, would no doubt favour a Strine Bible.

Day the Grog Ran Out and Other Stories from the Big Book and received the official endorsement of the Catholic Church. The temptation of Christ by the Devil went like this:

The day after the baptising bit, Jesus choofed off on his own into the desert. He stayed there 40 days and 40 nights and knocked off eating tucker so he could do some deep concentrated pondering. A particularly mean sort of heavy turned up to annoy Jesus. Knowing Jesus's tummy was doing a bit of a rumble, this heavy said that if Jesus was the Number One, all he had to do was whack on a bit of magic and turn a few chunks of rock into bread. Jesus said no way – man can't live proper with just bread; real living is hearing the words of God.

An even more extreme version, which every established church ran from as if it had measles, was produced in 1976 by Australian actor Bill Lyle. His version of 'The Feeding of the Five Thousand' went:

G'day. 'Ave you 'eard about the day Jesus and His mother had been working flat out with this big mob, curing warts and leprosy and all that? After a while the Apostles said: 'It's time to tie on the feed bag – but there's not enough tucker for this mob.'

Andrew said: 'Here's a kid with five loaves of bread and two fishes.' So Jesus said: 'Righto, bring me the bread and the bream.' He blesses it, breaks it into bits and the Apostles take it around.

Jesus said: 'Collect what's left over, or we'll be in strife for littering.' They found there was 12 baskets of food left over. Jesus had fed 5,000 blokes – that's not counting all the sheilas and kids.

Even though Ambrose Bierce may have called slang 'the speech of him who robs literary garbage cans on their way to the dumps', it is so important to the understanding of Australia, and therefore of Paul Hogan, that a little linguistic tuition has been included in this book. It will be noted that Australian slang contains many references to sex and drinking, but that perhaps is a subject for historians and students of Freud, and is of no concern here.

Glossary

Air raid: to argue loudly or scold.

Alley up: to pay up.

Amber fluid or nectar: beer.

Amen snorter: a clergyman.

Aristotle: a bottle (rhyming slang).

Artichoke: a debauched old woman.

Aunty: the Australian Broadcasting Commission; an ageing homosexual.

Australian salute: the movement made in brushing away flies from the face.

Axle grease: money.

Back of beyond: a remote area; also back of Bourke.

Bag: to criticize sarcastically ('He's always bagging politicians').

Bagman: person who collects bribes, usually for the police or for politicians.

Ball-tearer: something extremely good ('It was a ball-tearer of a party').

Bang: sexual intercourse.

Bare-bum: dinner-jacket.

Barrel: to beat up ('He insulted me so I barrelled him').

Bash: a party; sexual intercourse; attempt, as in 'have a bash'.

Bathers: swimsuit.

Beaut: the best.

Biff: punch.

Blind: drunk.

Blow-in: unexpected visitor.

Blue: a fight; mistake ('He made a blue and it turned into a blue').

Boiler: an older woman.

Bollicky: naked.

Bomb: an old car.

Bonzer: excellent.

Boofhead: a simpleton.

Booze: liquor; thus boozer [pub], booze-up [drinking session], booze artist [heavy drinker].

Bot: to borrow continually ('He bot me for a cigarette again').

Brasco: lavatory.

Brewer's droop: unable to get an erection, as a result of drinking too much alcohol.

Buckley's chance: no chance at all ('You've got Buckley's chance of passing the exam').

Buckshee: free.

Bumnut: an egg.

Bunfight: a crowded, noisy party.

Bung: broken; also used for temperamental behaviour, as in 'bung it on'; and putting on airs and graces, as in 'bung on'.

Burl: an attempt ('I'll give it a burl').

Bushman's clock: a kookaburra.

Butcher's hook: rhyming slang for crook (ill).

Cackleberries: eggs.

Captain Cook: a look (rhyming slang).

Cark: to die.

Charlie: a woman; also woman's breast ('That Charlie's got beaut Charlies').

Chew and spew: a cheap café.

Chook: a hen; also a woman, usually used affectionately ('You silly old chook').

Choppers: teeth.

Chuck: to vomit.

Clink: jail.

Clobber: to hit someone; also clothing ('He criticized my clobber so I clobbered him').

Cocky: farmer.

Crash: to pass out; sleep; a place to sleep; to go to a party or function uninvited or without paying ('I crashed the party but I had too much to drink and crashed').

Croak: to die.

Crumpet: a woman; also sexual favours.

Curry: to abuse someone ('I gave him curry over the mess he left'.)

Dag: a droll person.

Daks: trousers.

Dead marines: empty bottles.

Dead set: absolutely sure.

Dekko: a look, as in 'taking a dekko'.

Demon: a policeman.

Derro: a derelict, a no-hoper.

Dickless Tracy: a policewoman.

Ding: party; also to damage, usually used of motor vehicles ('After the ding I dinged the car').

Dinkum (also dinky-di): the genuine article ('Paul Hogan is a fair dinkum Australian').

Divvy: a dividend or share.

Dobber: a betrayer, informer.

Dogbox: trouble ('He got home late last night and now he's in the dogbox').

Dole: unemployment benefit.

Done: to be overcharged or cheated ('I was done like a dinner over the bill').

Dong: to hit.

Dope: stupid person; drugs.

Drongo: a born loser (named after a horse that always ran a place in important races but could never win).

Drum: brothel; the real facts ('Okay, sergeant, give me the drum on the drum').

Dubbo: silly person, fool.

Dudder: swindler or cheat; seller of shoddy goods.

Duffer: a cattle thief.

Dunny: a toilet.

Dust-up: a minor fight.

Earbash: to bore.

Earn: money earned by using wits.

Earwig: an eavesdropper; to eavesdrop.

Easy: susceptible to giving a loan or being swindled.

Elephants: drunk (rhyming slang for elephant's trunk).

Emu: one who haunts racecourses picking up discarded betting tickets in the hope of finding a good one.

Endless belt: a prostitute.

Esky: a portable cooler for carrying drinks.

Even stephens: equal shares ('We'll go even stephens on the bill').

Ex: a former husband or wife.

Extra: extraordinarily good.

Fair go: decent chance ('Give him a fair go').

Fang: borrow money ('He put the fangs into me again').

Fartsack: bed.

Ferret: penis.

Fizzgig: a police informer.

Flake: to sleep, especially if overcome by strong liquor.

Flap: to talk at length ('She didn't stop flapping her gums').

Flit: to leave a place, usually an apartment and usually at night, without paying ('He didn't have the rent so he did a moonlight flit').

Flyblown: without money, broke.

Freckle: anus.

Front: impudence, cheek ('He had more front than a department store').

Fruitcake: mad, insane.

Full: intoxicated ('He was as full as a family po [chamber pot]').

Funny business: sexual intercourse.

Furphy: a rumour.

Fuzz: police.

Gab: to talk idly.

Gaga: stupid; also besotted ('He's gone gaga over that girl').

Galah: a fool, idiot.

Galoot: an awkward, silly fellow.

Gander: a look, peek ('Take a gander at this').

Gargle: a drink.

Gasbag: an idle talker.

Ghost: a creditor, especially one who haunts for payment.

Gizzard: stomach.

Good sort: an attractive person.

Goog: an egg.

Goomie: a hopeless drunk, drinker of methylated spirits.

Graft: hard work.

Gravy: a perk, or money easily acquired.

Grizzle: to complain; a grizzle-guts is a persistent complainer.

Grotty: dirty, unattractive.

Grouse: good ('Thanks – that was an extra grouse feed').

Gurgler: plughole, used in reference to something irretrievably lost ('Every cent I had went down the gurgler on that horse').

Gyp: to swindle.

Hairy-legs: an expression of contempt.

Hambone: a male striptease, sometimes performed at surf life-saving clubs when the booze is flowing.

Hard case: a tough person (often used if he is amusing as well).

Hay: money; bed.

Head 'em: to toss the coins in a two-up game.

Hide: impudence or cheek ('You've got a hide selling me that tough steak').

Hitched: married.

Hoon: a pimp.

Hot: stolen; unreasonable or excessive ('It was a bit hot selling me hot stuff').

Humdinger: a remarkable thing or person.

Hump the bluey: to carry a swag.

Humpy: a small shack.

Hungry: mean or selfish.

Hunky-dory: satisfactory ('Everything's hunky-dory').

Hurl: to vomit.

Husband-beater: a long, narrow loaf of bread.

Iceberg: a person who swims in winter.

Icky: tricky.

Identity: a well-known character.

Illywhacker: a confidence trickster.

Incoherent: blind drunk.

Ink: cheap liquor.

Irish hurricane: dead calm.

Jack: a policeman; also venereal disease (the treatment clinic being called 'The House that Jack Built').

Jackass: a kookaburra.

Jack and Jill: bill (rhyming slang)

Jackeroo: male cattle or sheep-station hand.

Jack up: to refuse to proceed.

Jailbait: girls under the legal age for sex.

Jake: all right ('She'll be jake').

Jammy: requiring no effort, lucky ('That was jammy, finding that $20 note').

Jiffy: short time ('Hang on a jiffy').

Jilleroo: female station hand.

Jimjams: extremely nervous.

Jimmy Woodser: lone drinker.

Job: to punch.

Joey: a baby kangaroo.

John: a cop.

Joint: house or place of work ('How about coming back to my joint?').

Jug: prison.

Jumbuck: a sheep.

Jump: a head start, a good beginning ('I got to work early to get the jump on the others').

Jungle bunny: a black person (offensive: used only by whites).

Kadoova: deranged ('He was off his kadoova').

Kanga: wages.

Kibosh: to put a stop to some activity ('I put the kibosh on his plans').

Kick: pocket.

Kickapoo juice: illicit home-brewed liquor.

Kick on: to get ahead.

Kick the bucket: to die.

Kip: sleep; also thin piece of wood used for spinning coins in two-up game.

Knackered: tired.

Knee-trembler: act of sexual intercourse standing up.

Knock: to criticize ('He's always knocking the government').

Knockabout: one who makes out as best he can; an itinerant person.

Knockers: breasts.

Knuckle: a blow with the fist ('He got out of control so I gave him a knuckle sandwich').

Kremlin charlady: female of left-wing tendencies.

Lair: a flashily dressed young man of brash and vulgar behaviour ('He was nothing but a two-bob lair').

Larrikin: a street tough or hoodlum; rough and ready character; now used for independent person with little regard for authority.

Left-footer: a Roman Catholic.

Lemon: something that doesn't work ('The car he sold me was a lemon').

Lid: a hat.

Lingo: language ('Mind your lingo, there's ladies present').

Loaf: to do nothing ('He loafed about all day at work').

Lob: to arrive ('I lobbed at Fred's place at midnight').

Lodgings: jail.

Log: a person with few brains.

Long paddock: the open road, often used by graziers in times of drought.

Long shot: an outsider in a horse race.

Looksee: a visual examination.

Lousy: mean ('He was so lousy he wouldn't give away a homing pigeon').

Lout: rough, often violent, young man.

Lurgy: an infectious illness, such as influenza ('I've got the dreaded lurgy').

Lurk: a shady scheme ('Fred had a nice little lurk selling hot goods at the pub').

Macaroni: nonsense.

Mag: to talk idly ('She's been magging all day').

Mail: information ('Have you got any mail for this race?').

Make: to seduce.

Makings: the materials (papers, tobacco) to roll your own cigarette.

Mangy: mean ('He's a mangy bastard').

Mate: a friend, comrade.

**Perce the Wino – goomie and stalwart of the
Hogan TV shows – greets the world after a
refreshing night's sleep.**

Measly: something small; of bad quality ('That was a measly meal').

Melon: a fool.

Middy: standard glass of beer in New South Wales.

Mix it: to have a fight.

Mob: any large number of people or things ('There was a big mob at Fred's party').

Mocker: to bring bad luck ('Don't go to the races with Fred. He puts the mocker on you').

Monster: to harass persistently.

Moral: a certainty ('This horse is a moral to win').

Motser: a large amount of money, usually won gambling.

Muff: the female pudendum; also to bungle something.

Mug: a stupid person ('Stop acting like a mug').

Mulga: the outback.

Mullock: anything without value.

Munga: food.

Murder: a laborious, difficult task ('Doing my tax return is murder').

Musical milk: methylated spirits.

Mutt: a mongrel dog; a stupid person.

Mystery bag: a sausage.

Nag: a horse.

Nark: a spoilsport.

Naughty: sexual intercourse.

Necessary: money ('Have you got the necessary for a drink?').

Never-never: remote outback; also hire purchase ('I bought the car on the never-never').

New chum: a novice.

Nick: prison; also, to take off from work before schedule.

Nip: to borrow money ('He put the nip on me for $10').

Nipper: small boy.

Noah's Ark: rhyming slang for shark.

Nod: credit ('He let me buy it on the nod').

No-hoper: A useless person ('Fred's a right no-hoper').

Nong: a stupid person.

Norks: breasts (from Norco butter, the packaging of which featured a picture of a cow's udder).

Nosey-parker: a person who pries.

Nosh: to eat.

Nuddy: nude.

Nuff-nuff: a person with a speech impediment.

Nut ducker: a person who avoids others.

Ocker: a generally uncultured but usually good fellow; humorous, helpful, resourceful; user of slang.

Ockerina: female ocker.

Oil: useful information ('I've got the good oil on it').

Oldies: parents.

Old woman: the wife.

Oncer: one dollar.

Oodles: a lot, a plentiful supply ('He's got oodles of money').

Overlander: a drover who takes stock long distances through the outback.

Owled: drunk.

Oxford: a dollar (rhyming slang for Oxford scholar).

Oz: Australia.

Pad: residence.

Paddymelon: a small wallaby.

Pakapoo ticket: something written in an incomprehensible manner.

Parachute: a fart.

Paralytic: dead drunk ('Fred got paralytic at the party').

Pasting: a beating in a fight ('He took a pasting').

Peanut: idiot.

Pearler: excellent.

Percy: penis (to 'point Percy at the porcelain' is to urinate).

Perish: usually applied to death from dehydration in the outback ('The poor bugger did a perish when he ran out of water').

Perk: a side benefit ('With this job you get goods wholesale as a perk').

Perve: to look admiringly at a female, but not in an unsavoury manner.

Pickings: the cream of any deal.

Picnic: a good time; but a nice picnic can mean something unpleasant ('That's a nice picnic you've got us into now').

Piece of cake: easy ('The job was a piece of cake').

Piker: one who through lack of courage pulls out of a project.

Pin: a leg.

Piss: to urinate; also rain, booze; past tense, drunk ('pissed') or disgruntled ('pissed off').

Pisspot: a drunk.

Plonk: cheap wine.

Pluck: to rob or fleece.

Poke: to hit a person with a fist; act of sexual intercourse.

Pokies: poker, or slot, machines.

Pommy: an English person.

Pong: unpleasant smell.

Poofter: a male homosexual.

Pork: the police force.

Possie: a position or place ('This is a good possie to watch the game').

Port: suitcase.

Poultice: large amount of money.

Prang: accident.

Proverbial: elusive money ('He was always searching for the proverbial' e.g. proverbial dollar').

Puke: to vomit.

Pull: a lot of influence ('Fred had a lot of pull with the city council').

Punt: to bet.

Push: a gang of larrikins, louts.

Quandong: a woman who refuses to have sex after being wined and dined.

Quickie: something done in a short space of time, including a brief sexual encounter.

Quid: one pound, now two dollars; used mostly in describing a mentally defective person as 'not being the full quid'.

Quince: a male homosexual.

Quoit: buttocks; also spelled coit.

Racehorse: a thinly rolled cigarette.

Rafferty's Rules: no rules at all.

Rag: a newspaper.

Rapt: delighted, infatuated ('He's rapt in her').

Ratbag: an eccentric person, a rascal.

Razoo: a non-existent brass coin (used in the expression 'he hasn't a brass razoo').

Razz: to deride, make fun of.

Ready: cash ('I've got enough ready for a round of drinks').

Ridgey-didge: the absolute truth.

Ring: the centre of operations in a two-up school; the anus.

Ringer: a stockman.

Ring-in: a substitute person or animal, usually a horse.

Ripped: drunk.

Ripper: something particularly good ('I had a ripper time last night').

Root: sexual intercourse.

Ropeable: angry.

Rort: a scheme, often shady; a party ('It was a good rort except Fred rorted us on the cost of booze').

Rough: unreasonable, unfair ('You were a bit rough on him').

Roughie: an outsider in a race.

Rouse: to castigate.

Rouseabout: a handyman on a property.

Rubbish: to speak ill of.

Rustle: to move quickly.

Sack: bed; to dismiss.

Saddle-up: to prepare for work.

Sanger: sandwich.

Scad: plenty ('He had a scad of money').

Scarper: to depart rapidly.

School: a group settled in for a drinking session.

Schooner: a glass of beer.

Scone: head.

Score: to borrow or win money ('I scored well at the races after I scored a loan from Fred').

Scrap: a fight.

Screw: wages; a prison warder; the act of sexual intercourse.

Scunge: dirt, garbage.

Septic tank: rhyming slang for Yank, usually shortened to septic.

Set: to be certain of a successful endeavour ('I'm set like a jelly on that horse').

Shag: to fornicate.

Sharkbait: a swimmer who ventures too far out to sea.

Sheila: a female.

Sherbet: beer.

Shickered: drunk.

Shindig: a party, especially a noisy one.

Shirt-lifter: a male homosexual.

Shouse: a lavatory (shit-house), or something not very good ('That was a shouse meal').

Shout: turn to buy a drink.

Shrapnel: small change.

Shunt: to get rid of someone whose company you no longer want.

Sickie: a day taken off work, whether sick or not ('I think I'll throw a sickie and go to the beach').

Skirt: a woman or girl.

Skite: to boast.

Slash: to urinate.

Slime: to crawl, curry favour.

Sling: to bribe ('I had to sling the cop $50 to let me off').

Sly grog: illegal alcohol.

Smoko: a short tea-break at work.

Snags: sausages.

Snake gully: mythical country area.

Snip: to borrow money.

Snow drop: to steal from a clothes-line in someone's backyard.

Souvenir: to steal ('I think I'll souvenir a few hotel ash-trays').

Sparrowfart: crack of dawn ('I'm tired. I've been up since sparrowfart').

Spiel: glib or plausible talk.

Spliced: married.

Sponger: a freeloader.

Sprog: a young child.

Squib: to evade an issue.

Squiffy: askew; slightly drunk.

Squint: furtive glance ('Take a quick squint at her').

Stonkered: drunk.

Strewth: exclamation of surprise ('Strewth, you wouldn't believe it'), from 'God's truth'.

Strides: trousers.

Stroppy: argumentative.

Stuff: to have sexual intercourse; usually used as an insulting remark ('Go and get stuffed').

Suckhole: a crawler.

Suss: something unreliable needing confirmtion ('It sounds a bit suss to me'), from 'suspect'.

Swag: a bundle or roll of belongings; a large amount ('Fred's got a fair swag of kids').

Sweet: satisfied ('That deal we made is sweet').

Swish: stylish, glamorous ('That's a swish outfit you're wearing').

Swy: two-up gambling game.

Tag: to follow closely.

Take: the profit from a quick business venture.

Tanked: drunk.

Tarpaulin muster: a collection at a gathering, usually to buy more booze.

Threads: clothes.

Tick: credit.

Tight: mean ('He's as tight as a shark's arse – and that's watertight').

Tinny: beer; also person who is unusually lucky ('Jeez, Fred's tinny at the races').

Toey: nervous, anxious to get going.

Tomtits: diarrhoea; anger; being fed up ('This bloke's giving me the tomtits') (rhyming slang).

Top-off: an informer.

Traps: familiar places such as clubs and pubs ('I reckon I'll go round the traps for a while').

Trimmer: something exceptionally good ('The sheila I was out with last night's a little trimmer').

Tubes: cans of beer.

Tucker: food.

Tumble: to wake up to something ('I tumbled him right away').

Turps: alcohol.

Tweeds: trousers.

Twist: insane ('He's round the twist').

Two-bob: poor-quality ('My car goes like a two-bob watch').

Two-up: gambling game in which two pennies are thrown in the air; also known as swy.

Uncle: a pawnbroker.

Underdaks: underpants.

Underground mutton: rabbit.

Upya: an offensive exclamation, used most often as in 'Upya for the rent'.

Urger: racecourse tout.

Ute: abbreviation of utility truck.

Vag: a vagrant.

Vegetable: a boring, dull person.

Verbal: a verbal confession made to the police which is alleged to be fabricated.

Verbal diarrhoea: a lot of (spoken) nonsense.

Visiting card: something left behind which is immediately recognizable as belonging to a certain person ('Fred's dog left his visiting card').

Wad: a large roll of money.

Wake-up: alert ('Don't try and pit it over me. I'm wake-up to you').

Walkabout: wandering around an area ('I think I'll go walkabout').

Walloper: a policeman.

Wank: originally masturbate, but now used mostly to denote egotistical or self-indulgent behaviour.

Wanker: a deluded fool ('That politician is a wanker').

Warb: a derelict person.

Wet: a simpleton; The Wet is the rainy season in Northern Australia.

Whack: a ration, share ('I want my fair whack out of the deal').

What's all this then? Hoges as a Pommy walloper.

Whacko: a cry of pleasure, as in 'whacko-the-diddle-oh'.

Whatnot: no matter what, anything.

Whinge: to complain constantly.

White ant: to sabotage ('That bastard's been trying to white ant me at work').

Windbag: a garrulous but empty talker.

Wing-ding: a party.

Wino: an alcoholic.

Wood: the advantage ('You've got the wood on me').

Woofters: the dog races.

Woop Woop: any remote area.

Works: everything ('Come on team, give them the works').

Yabber: to chatter.

Yakka: hard work.

Yamma: to complain.

Yobbo: a lout.

Yonks: a long time ('I haven't seen Fred for yonks').

Yucky: unpleasant ('That's yucky grub').

Yummy: very good ('The grub is yummy').

Zack: sixpence, now five cents.

Ziff: beard.

Zizz: a short sleep.

Zonked: exhausted, drunk.

Zot: to knock out or kill quickly ('Zot that fly').

'*The phenomenon of laughter has attracted the attention of thinkers through the ages – and rightly so. For the role of humour as a safety valve and an aid in meeting adversity with a minimum of fuss has surely earned it a niche in any worthwhile philosophy of life.*'

Keith Willey

Jenny Howard was a popular singer on the British and Australian variety stages in the 'thirties and 'forties. Born in Britain, she was a gentle person and if her friends had ever been asked to describe her they would probably have said 'ladylike'. Therefore she was somewhat startled when in Melbourne in 1940 she was introduced to the man who was to be her co-star for a ten-week season at the Tivoli Theatre. He looked nothing like a co-star. In fact, he looked nothing like anyone she had ever met. She recalled:

This strange apparition walked through the door and held me spellbound. He looked very rugged and I don't think he had shaved. His tie had stains on it and his clothes had cigarette ash all over them. But what really fascinated me was I'd never seen anyone keep his trousers up without braces before. He had this enormous stomach and his pants were somewhere beneath his stomach. He croaked in a funny voice, 'I'm Wallace. I'm a natural lair.'

Having never heard the word I thought perhaps he was an Aboriginal. In my best British accent I said, 'How do you do?' He said, 'I'm all right. I'm a bit rough in the morning.'

And I thought, 'So he's a bit rough in the morning and he's a lair. I suppose it will work out somehow.'

She had just met George Wallace, one of Australia's most popular comedians, and it did work out. Nancye Bridges, in her book *Curtain Call* (with Frank Crook, 1980), described Wallace as 'looking like a wharf labourer who had lifted one bale too many . . . He had short legs, arms that seemed too long for his body and an accent that sounded like pebbles being poured into an empty bucket.' Wallace was one in a long line of Australian larrikin comedians, of which Paul Hogan is the latest and arguably most successful. The dag standing in the corner, beer in one hand, cigarette in the other, commenting laconically on life, firmly opposed to all authority, detesting all politicians, especially those he helped put in power, happiest when his football team is winning, on familiar terms with his boss and bank manager and friendly with at least one football player or jockey, mildly intolerant of all nationalities but especially New Zealanders, revering Don Bradman, Les Darcy and anyone who has beaten the Taxation Department, able to strip his Holden car to the axles and assemble it again before lunch but incapable of mending the lawnmower, suspicious of too much education, except for that of his own kids, speaking the language of the suburbs . . . this is the character with whom Australians can identify. Hogan, with a few variations, portrays that character.

I have called Hogan a larrikin comedian and it should be explained that larrikin was once an offensive description. H. Furniss, author of *Australian Sketches* (1888), saw many larrikins in old Sydney town and was appalled. He gave this description:

In Sydney he is a 'chartered libertine', and suffers little molestation from the law, though he freely molests law-abiding citizens. Individually, he is a low, loafing sneak and a thorough coward . . . The larrikin has nothing manly about him. He is a sharp, active, horsey-looking, vicious cad; he rarely does any work, but mostly lives upon the lowest means possible – by the vice of others . . . a glance at any of them shows clearly the immature criminal, and, also, alas! that for such there can be no future but that of social pests and vermin. This feature is the darkest blot upon Australian society, and upon Sydney in particular. It is strange that, with an immense body of clerical and lay workers in every branch of mission work, this evil should be so rampant and unchecked.

The meaning of the word has changed. The *Macquarie Dictionary* defines 'larrikin' as 'a mischievous young person'. A larrikin can now be described as someone who snubs his nose at authority, who bends and sometimes breaks the rules but means harm to no one – the boy caught with his hand in the cookie jar, the man caught in the pub trying to chat up an unresponsive barmaid.

Larrikinism has strongly influenced Australian humour. While devoid of the classical references or flowing phrases that might be found in the delivery of comics from say, an Oxford or Cambridge University background, it is likewise lacking in the brittle satire of the colder climes of Europe and the glib, polished lines that slip so easily from the lips of the Hollywood greats. If Australian humour can be compared to any it probably comes closest to the dry pessimism of the north of England. Someone who knows about Australian humour is Dorothy Jones, head of the University of Wollongong's English department. Having spent two years studying the subject, she concluded that if Australian humour came from anywhere it was from the harsh environment of the bush.

The pattern is that of being up against it, that things are so bad you can only laugh. There's a quality about it saying you can't win, and it's a protest against the monotony and harshness of existing in a hostile environment. Our humour is quite sombre and there's a certain bleakness about it. You hear it in the very laconic statements. Saying things like 'he throws money around like a man with no hands' tends to cut people down somewhat. Another example would be a joke from World War I when an Aussie soldier was piggy-backing his wounded comrade out of the battlefield. The wounded man says: 'Hey, what about turning around and walking backwards for a while? You're going to get the VC [Victoria Cross] and I'm getting all the flamin' bullets.'

Keith Willey, in *You Might As Well Laugh, Mate* (1984), says much the same thing.

Unlike some noted larrikins, Hoges has never had any problems mixing with aristos (Hogan pictured here with Jeanette Charles).

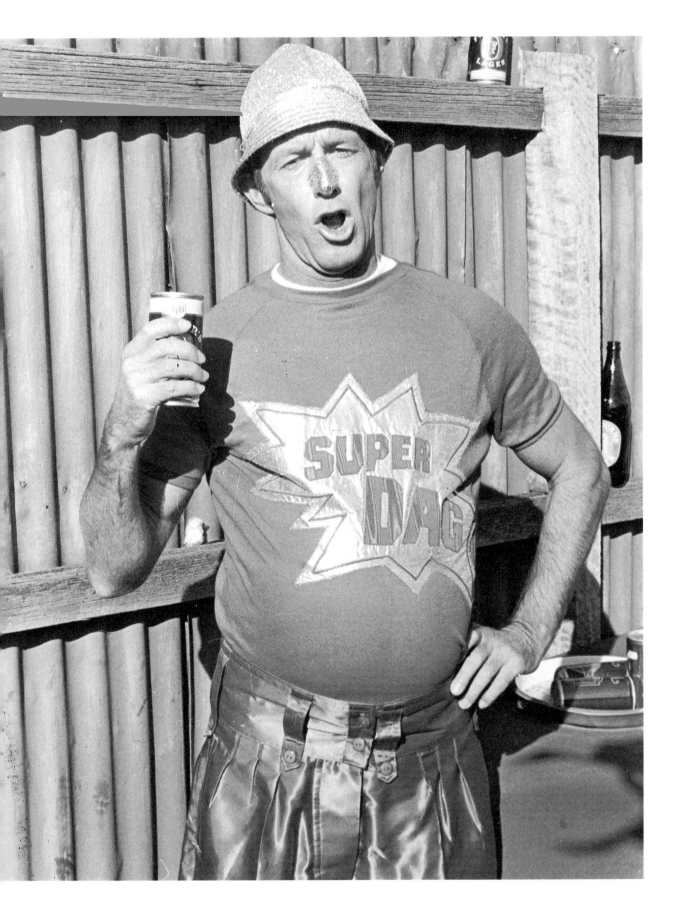

The pioneers and those who followed found their ultimate foe not in other men but in climate and geography. Gradually and painfully they learned to co-exist with their environment rather than seek to conquer it outright. As a result the national mood became one of stoic acceptance, reflected in a style of humour as dry as a desert claypan.

He cited an example he called The Great Australian Joke. Two old swaggies had been wandering through the backblocks together for many years. Early one morning they passed the carcass of a large animal, black and swollen.

Around midday one of the swaggies, Bill, took his pipe from his mouth and grunted, 'D'yer see that dead ox?'

That night, around a campfire, the other swaggie, Jim, said, ' 'Tweren't an ox. 'Twas an 'orse.' He then turned in and slept for eight hours.

When he awoke there was no sign of his mate – only a grimy note stuck in a cleft stick. The note said: 'There's too much argyment in this 'ere camp.'

Of course, one man's joke is another man's puzzled expression. But humorist Buzz Kennedy's selection for the great Australian joke is worth repeating. It involved a squatter (a large landowner) in the Depression of the 'thirties. To his annoyance, neighbouring cow-cockies (small landowners) were forever pulling his outer gates to pieces for the nuts and bolts, which held the timbers together, that they couldn't afford to buy.

Finally, he put boxes of mixed nuts and bolts by each gate, with a notice: 'Take what you want.'

The next time he made his rounds, bits of the first gate he came to were scattered everywhere. And across his notice was scrawled: 'Keep your bloody charity.'

There wasn't much to laugh about when Australia was first settled in the eighteenth century, mostly by British and Irish convicts who had been transported – often for minor offences or political reasons. They couldn't find many jokes in the new continent, or much to tickle the ribs, especially if they were caught

Super Dag – the beer-swilling loudmouth who haunts most of the world's watering-holes.

breaking even the most minor of rules. An eyewitness account of the type of punishment inflicted almost daily is provided by T. Crofton Croker in *Memoirs of Joseph Holt*:

The next prisoner who was tied up was Paddy Galvin, a young lad of about 20 years of age; he was also sentenced to receive 300 lashes. The first 100 were given on his shoulders, and he was cut to the bone between the shoulder blades, which were both bare. The doctor then directed the next hundred to be inflicted lower down, which reduced his flesh to such a jelly that the doctor ordered him to have the remaining 100 on the calves of his legs. During the whole time Galvin never even whimpered or flinched, if, indeed, it had been possible for him to have done so . . . He was put into the cart and sent to the hospital.

Such treatment was not likely to have the early inhabitants rolling in the aisles. The free settlers were not much better off; years of drought could end in floods, followed by a bushfire and perhaps a plague of grasshoppers coupled with a disease that could wipe out stock and crops. Then there were snakes, venomous spiders, leeches, ticks and flies – gawd, the flies – and mobs of kangaroos, later rabbits, that viewed the young, sweet pastures the way a hungry man might a groaning table. Good grief, even the birds could be dangerous – a kick from the leg of a cassowary, a native of north-east Australia, could break a man's bones. The days could be like a furnace and the nights as cold as a whore's kiss.

The country lay in wait to destroy any who showed weakness. The men, and women, were tough because they had to be. There was little time for refinement; silk did not stand up to the bush like cowhide and polite words were no substitute for a string of oaths when faced with mud one day and powdery dust the next. Maybe Governor Lachlan Macquarie was right when he said in 1822: 'There are only two classes of persons in New South Wales – those who have been convicted and those who ought to have been.'

After casting an eye over the early colony, Richard Horne, in *Australian Facts and Prospects* (1859), went further.

The young men . . . have no relish for learning or philosophy, or science, no taste for reading anything but trash, or seeing anything on the stage but burlesque, and no ruling impulse with respect to literature, the fine arts, manners, the respect and delicacy due to ladies, and personal habits . . . and self-command in smoking and drinking . . . but desecration. The majority possess no educational knowledge, no talents or taste, and they cordially hate all those who do possess such acquirements.

Perhaps Britain was partially to blame for this attitude. It is an idea favoured by the Australian writer Thomas Keneally, winner of the prestigious Booker Prize for literature, who in the *Sydney Morning Herald* said in in 1987:

My theory of Australian history is that the reasons we are such yobbos and such unbuttoned, boozing hoons is that we're Georgian. The eighteenth-century Englishmen were like this. They were great topers and they gambled on everything. Italians used to go to London and say the English were too emotional! There was an accessibility of politicians and royalty, like the mad king himself, which operates with Australian cabinet ministers and politicians. Anybody can go up and say, 'G'day, Bob [Prime Minister Bob Hawke], how yer going?' I'm sure it's where the Australian reputations for wildness on the one hand, and anarchy and conservatism on the other, come from.

Another reason was that in the Colony there was little time for the activities Richard Horne found so desirable. Survival was all that mattered. But as the settlement grew and flourished a national humour emerged, even if it was edged with despair and shadowed by the gallows, echoed in an old bush saying: 'You might as well laugh, mate – there's nothing else to do.'

Pioneers carving properties from the bush had much to complain about, but they often did it in a sardonic, understated way. A 1913 cartoon says it best:

Sunday-school teacher: 'And it rained for 40 days and 40 nights.'
Smart lad: 'An' was the cockies satisfied then?'

The appalling early conditions unfortunately produced a cruel side to the Australian character which, coupled with a racist attitude inherited from Britain, proved deadly to the Aboriginal people. They were slaughtered. In Tasmania, for instance, the Aborigines were reduced from 4,000 in 1803, when the British set up a colony, to none in 1876. The Aborigines were killed in a way so brutal and savage it would have pleased the Third Reich or Pol Pot. Men and children were emasculated and mutilated; their flesh was fed to the dogs; babies were flung on to campfires; men were brained with stones and clubs. White settlers considered it an amusing day's sport, akin to shooting rabbits or wallabies, to hunt and kill a few blacks. The cruelty was sometimes reflected in the humour, especially in early slapstick comedy. Keith Willey, in *You Might As Well Laugh, Mate*, argues that the cruelty underlying some of the slapstick comedy may have been essential to the success of early settlers, especially those who worked small farms. 'They provided comic relief from the experiences of small selectors late last century. At the same time they emphasized the brutal hardness and frequent heartbreak of the life.' Professor A.D. Hope says much the same thing: 'If the humour sometimes seems a bit cruel it is because that is the humour that keeps people going in desperate circumstances – and the same applies to the comic exaggeration. Only by making it absurd can you laugh away fear and horror.'

What the harsh conditions did was create, if not a classless society, at least one in which the strata were not as rigidly defined as they were in Europe. Nature made no distinction between the wealthy and the poor, between those who owned tracts of land the size of England and those who possessed only the rags on their backs – all were fair game. Today the worker drinks with his boss, the only difference being that the latter could well be the one dressed in singlet and shorts. Bill Hornadge, in *The Australian Slanguage*, quotes British comedian Harry Secombe on the subject, using as illustration the fact that in Australia a male passenger who sits in the back of a taxi in preference to riding up front with the driver could be regarded as 'putting on airs'. Said Secombe: 'The first time I was [in Australia] I hopped into the back seat of a Sydney taxi and the driver asked me if I had leprosy.' Hornadge also relates the story of the president of the Victorian Football League who was attending a luncheon in Sydney as a guest speaker. The luncheon was self-serve and the president, standing in the queue, asked the steward for an extra dob of butter. He was told there was only one per person. The following conversation then took place:

President: 'Do you know who I am?'
Steward: 'No.'
President: 'Well, I'm the president of the Victorian Football League and your guest speaker today. Do you think I could have two dobs of butter?'
Steward: 'Do you know who I am?'
President: 'You have me at a disadvantage there. I don't know.'
Steward: 'Well, I'm the guy who dishes out the bloody butter.'

The great Depression of the 'thirties, during which Australia became a nation of gypsies searching for work, brought Australian humour even closer to the gallows. Thomas Wood, in *Cobbers* (1934), related this story:

It is a tale of the Gap, a cliff near the South Head [Sydney] which offers such a deep, clean drop from this world into another that all the best suicides gave it their patronage . . .
And when the policeman got up to the man he was sitting on the very edge, all ready. 'What's up, digger?' asked the policeman.
'Everything,' said the man. 'This Depression's got me down. The wife's run off with a cobber o' mine; the shop's gone to the pack; the kid's crook and I've lost me false teeth.'
'Gow-orn!' said the policeman sympathetically.
'So I'm going over the Gap,' said the man, and pulled off his coat.
'You may be,' said the policeman, soothing him, 'but we'll have to talk about it first.'
So they had a talk about it first. Then they both went over the Gap.

Another joke, known to most Australians, came out of that bleak period. A waterside worker fell off the wharf and was drowning. Noticing this, an unemployed man rushed to the foreman and asked for the job of the fellow, who was still struggling weakly in the water. 'You're too late,' he was told. 'I've given it to the bloke who pushed him in.'

But the Depression produced great larrikin comedians such as George Wallace and, funniest of them all, Roy 'Mo' Rene. Even when fighting for survival, Australians did not begrudge a few pence to see Roy Rene on stage. The variety entertainer Queenie Ashton recalled the time she appeared on the same bill as Rene but was worried that few patrons would turn up because of the Depression.

When we walked around the corner, I'll never forget this sight as long as I live. There was a queue right away up to near the Lyric Theatre. Right up George Street [Sydney] and there was a crowd on the road and the police were pushing them off. So Mike [her husband] went up to the queue and said, 'How do you fellows make ends meet?' and they said, 'Oh, cor blimey, we can always spend a shilling out of the dole to come in and forget our troubles; forget everything to have a laugh and see Mo.'

Born in Adelaide in 1892 (his real name was Harry van de Sluice), Rene entered show business at the age of eight, when he played the part of a duck in the pantomime *Sinbad the Sailor*. His father, a keen race-goer, was not pleased because he thought his son would have a better career as a jockey. When the family moved to Melbourne, Rene got a job at the Gaiety Theatre as a boy soprano. His father tried new tactics to dissuade him from a stage career. Each night he packed the audience with friends who gave his son 'the raspberry' – relays of them, booing and hooting, trying to undermine the boy's confidence. The scheme failed, and when his voice broke, at fifteen, Rene donned a red nose and became a comedian.

Rene later applied black greasepaint to his face, like an exaggerated five o'clock shadow, and became the Jewish comedian Mo. His was an Australian humour which could have travelled overseas except that the world was not ready for larrikins from Down Under. The journalist Roland Pullen said in 1944: 'Roy Rene's humour is foreign to the cerebral humour of Groucho Marx and quite independent of scripts. Unconscious as Mo may be in his approach to humour, he is really representing an important part of Australian life.' Lord Beauchamp, a former Governor of New South Wales, used to go to see Rene twice a week. On returning to England he wrote Rene a letter which said: 'Your art is an important part of the Australian ethos.' Rene cracked back: 'Gorblimey, I hope that's a compliment.'

Rene always believed his humour was so

Hogan – larrikin cabbie? – pictured with a four-wheeled pride and joy that had perhaps seen better days.

Australian it might not be understood beyond his home shores. 'The people here understand me, I work in their language, my stuff is folklore stuff. I don't think I would go over anywhere else.' A New Zealand tour was not especially successful because the locals could barely understand him. 'Strike me lucky,' he said on his return, 'what could I say, boy? They're supposed to speak the King's English, aren't they?' Nor would he go to the United States, even though some handsome offers were made to him. 'Break it down,' he said. 'Look what happened to Les Darcy and Phar

Lap when they went to America [they died]. Strike me lucky, they might make it a treble.'

But some overseas visitors did understand his humour. During World War II, the American comedian Jack Benny saw Rene at the Tivoli Theatre, Sydney. After the performance, Benny turned to the show's producer, and said: 'I can't understand a word of what this guy's talking about, but he's one of the funniest men I've ever seen.' Dame Sybil Thorndike thought the same. She said that one day Australians would appreciate the fact that Rene was a comic genius. When told of this compliment, Rene said: 'That's very nice of the old sheila.'

Rene's act was a mixture of innocent lechery, lampooning of the prevailing prudish-

ness and the portrayal of the underdog trium-
phant against the odds, an appealing image at a
time when nearly one-third of the work force
was unemployed. One of his more famous
sketches was 'Golden Wedding', in which a
husband tells his butler how happy his married
life has been.

Butler: 'Sir, may I ask you a very personal question?'

Rene: 'Nothing rude, I hope, Carruthers?'

Butler: 'No, sir. It's just this – you and your
good lady have been married for 50 years, but you
have no children. Why is that, sir? Don't you like
children?'

Rene (with increasing pathos): 'I love children,
Carruthers, and it's a great sorrow to me that our
union was never blessed with little babies. But it all
dates back to 51 years ago, shortly before Mary and
I were married . . . We had gone for a stroll in the
park, we sat down on the grass, and I took her in
my arms. She looked so lovely, with the soft
moonlight shining down on her beautiful face –
something swept over me, and I whispered something to her.'

Butler: 'You did, sir?'

Rene: 'Yes, and she went so crook, I haven't
been game to mention it since.'

He delighted in annoying wowsers. In one
of his sketches he would write the letter F on a
blackboard. 'What's that, Stiffy?' he would
ask his straight man.

'It's K,' Stiffy would reply.

He did this several times, then would appear
to lose patience and snap: 'I don't know what's
wrong with you, Stiffy. Every time I write F,
you see K.' The famous four-letter word was
out in the open in mixed company at a time
when it was spoken only in pubs, on the
racetrack and in knocking shops.

Rene was best at ad-libbing, which frequently got him into trouble with the law. But
he always maintained it was not his fault if
people chose to laugh at the vulgar side of his
double-meaning jokes. One night a woman
singer who appeared with him was given a
bunch of flowers. Amid the clapping and
applause, Rene leered and said: 'Look at that!
Look at that! You get the flowers, and I get the
clap.'

Some of the colloquial expressions Paul
Hogan uses today come from Rene. He may
not have invented them but he popularized
them, though when asked where he picked up
phrases Rene would declare indignantly: 'Pick
them up? Pick them up? I didn't pick them
up, I originated them.' Among the expressions
he used were ratbag, galah, mug, dingo, strike
me lucky, one of my mob, you little trimmer, a
grouse sheila, you beauty, fair go, pull your
head in.

Rene was a larrikin both on and off stage.
For instance, he had a habit of stealing from
shops, mainly because he was convinced that
every store was out to rob him. Fred Parsons,
in *A Man Called Mo* (1973), recounted the
time he accompanied Rene on a shopping
expedition for a hat.

The salesman recognized him – most people did –
and laughed when he said, 'Good morning. I want a
hat.' The size, shape and desired colour of the hat
were given, and received with laughs, as if it was a
comedy routine, then the salesman said the hat
required was in a room at the back. Hardly before
he was out of sight, Roy turned to me, saying, 'The
mug's going to touch me because he knows I'm
Mo.' With that, he grabbed half-a-dozen ties off a
nearby rack, and stuffed them inside his shirt. He
bought that hat after getting a few shillings knocked off the price, happy that he had won a notable
victory over another 'mug'.

Like any good larrikin, he had little time for
pomposity or for the well-educated who dropped long words the way the average man might
swear. After being interviewed by Max Harris,
a self-appointed guardian of the language,
Rene said to Fred Parsons: 'He kept asking me
to explain the underlying psychology of me
comedy. Then he'd say something about
"social motivation". Fair dinkum, pal. I
didn't know what the mug was talking about.
He got me so rattled, I often gave him the
wrong steer.'

Roy Rene died in 1954.

If Rene was the epitome of the larrikin, the
ocker, on stage, Lennie Lower was his
counterpart in print. Throughout the 'thirties
and early 'forties he kept Australia, especially
Sydney, laughing as it read his work in newspapers and magazines. For years he turned out
a daily column of humour, which is regarded
as the most difficult task in journalism, and in
doing so he drank himself to death.

Lower reached his heights on the *Daily Telegraph*, owned by Frank (later Sir Frank) Packer, father of Kerry Packer, the man who for better or worse knocked the tradition out of cricket by changing it into a game for the masses like baseball. Lower didn't write at a desk, but in the pubs and clubs of central Sydney – a few paragraphs in one bar, a few more in another, sometimes scrawling the column on cigarette packets. As the deadline for his copy drew near, a search would be made of the various hostelries until he was located. Packer was forever sacking him on a Friday night for outrageous behaviour, then on Monday morning demanding he be found so he could be rehired.

It was on the night of a famous incident involving Noel Coward that Packer got rid of Lower for good. Lower was sent to cover a reception in Sydney Town Hall for the British theatrical personality, a task which irritated him because he disliked homosexuals and Coward was widely rumoured to be of that persuasion.

In due course Coward was introduced to Lower. 'Ah, the king of Australian humorists, one presumes,' said Coward in a condescending tone that made Lower furious.

'Ah, the great queen of the English stage, one presumes,' replied Lower.

Packer overheard the comment and angrily demanded an apology, Lower refused, was sacked and immediately hired by the editorially robust *Smith's Weekly*, which couldn't have cared less what a Pommy was called.

Lower detested wowsers, spearing them with his pen whenever the opportunity arose. One column summed up his attitude:

A Sydney clergyman, who has been indulging in the increasingly popular pastime of hunting for vice, says he saw 'revolting sights'.

As he was merely gathering evidence, he said, he did not wear his ecclesiastical collar.

I suppose it would be a bit of a drawback.

I wish I knew where all those places were. I don't have much fun these days, and I would be delighted to take off my collar and tie and, if necessary, my shirt, and be shown all the hot spots by some reverend gentleman.

Of course some people are very easily revolted. We could, perhaps, start off with a billiard saloon.

That is the second stage on the downward path, the first stage being playing dominoes in a coffee lounge during the lunch hour . . .

So-called Sydney society was on the receiving end of Lower's barbs, especially during the worst days of the Depression when some newspapers would record the activities of the wealthy as though it were important news. He wrote:

The charming home of Mr and Mrs John Bowyang, tucked away in Pelican Street, Surry Hills, is a revelation in piquancy. From the backyard one has a view of every other backyard, and the tall chimneystack of Tooth's Brewery looms majestically in the distance . . .

Mrs Bowyang's hobbies are washing and mending . . . Business takes Mr Bowyang away every morning at 6.30, he being engaged in the sewer-digging profession. But he still finds time for his diversions, namely, washing up and placing tins where the rain comes in. The younger children have a magnificent playground in Pelican Street, where they have a jolly time daubing themselves with mud, eating stray apple-cores, and escaping being run over by passing lorries.

Possibly not a popular figure today because of his chauvinistic attitude to women, Lower liked nothing more than drinking with his mates and could strike up an instant camaraderie with a drinking companion. He enjoyed knockabouts, describing in his column how he met one when booking into a country hotel.

'I want to book a room here,' I told him.

'Don't be silly,' he replied. 'Sleep out on the verandah with the rest of us if you've got blankets. They're decorating the School of Arts with the sheets. You going to the dance?'

'I can't dance.'

'Strike me pink, who wants to? We leave that to the women. There ought to be some good fights at this one. When I was younger there wasn't a man who could stand up to me on the dance floor.

When he died, the cartoonist W.E. Pidgeon said of him: 'His obituary is written, not in the newspapers, but in the trams, and the bars, and in the hearts of human men.'

Lennie Lower died in 1947. Out in the western suburbs of Sydney, in the heartland of the working classes, another larrikin was growing up.

Paul Hogan was then seven.

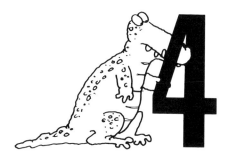

'*In those days I would just as soon smack someone in the ear as talk to him.*'
Paul Hogan

By a fortunate accident of life, Paul Hogan was born in Lightning Ridge. It gave him an advantage on people who began their lives in the more mundane Melbourne or Sydney, a name to drop with some satisfaction because there are few on this planet who have drawn their first breath in Lightning Ridge.

'Hey, mate, where were you born?'

'Lightning Ridge.'

'Cripes, I knew it, I always reckoned you came from the bush.'

'Yeah, but I left when I was a baby.'

No matter. When he was born on 8 October 1939, Lightning Ridge was – and for that matter, still is – a wild and woolly town where men of 40 nationalities tunnel down into rock for black opal, 'the finest opal in the world, in colours from aqua to magnificent deep red. Lying in the baking landscape of far north-west New South Wales, populated by about 1,500 (though there could be more because some residents disappear when heads are about to be counted), it is a place of secret deals, undisclosed surnames, suspicion of strangers in case they are employed by the Taxation Department, and violence. Shootings are not uncommon, especially over allegations of claim-jumping. Fortunes can be made in a day. As an Englishman, known by no other name than Oxford Terry, put it in 1987: 'You can make $100,000 tomorrow afternoon and nothing for the rest of your life. Some claims are so rich we call them "gun claims", because you need a gun to protect them.'

Hogan Senior, of Irish Catholic descent, ran a small transport business which included a postal delivery along tracks that should have been charged with fraud for calling themselves roads. Paul was 18 months old when the family left Lightning Ridge for Sydney, but he has always believed that somehow Lightning Ridge helped shape his life. Maybe it did. Maybe in the first months of his life he absorbed some of the independent air of Lightning Ridge – and some of its lawlessness. With an elder sister, Wendy, and a younger brother, Pat, he grew up in Granville, a sub-urb in the west of Sydney. His father worked here as a purchasing officer for the army. He died when Hogan was 20.

His father's early death was never forgotten by Hogan, who swore he would take advantage of life's opportunities and not wait around for events to happen: 'My old man fell down dead, still waiting for his world discovery tour. I decided not to wait.'

His brother Pat later settled in Canada, while his sister Wendy married Olympic swimmer John Devitt, gold medal winner of the 100-metre freestyle at the 1960 Rome Games and silver medal winner over the same distance at the 1956 Melbourne Games.

Granville was a working-class area of similar houses that faced each other up similar streets, not an unpleasant place in which to live but without an appealing style. The streets may have been wide, there may have been parks and the houses had large yards in which to kick or hit balls, but beyond that there was not a lot for kids. And furthermore the most important thing in life was far across the city. The most important thing in life was Sydney's string of beaches, where the sand was clean and the surf pounded so hard that the ground shook. 'Boring' would have been a reasonable description of Granville. Boring houses. Boring shops. Boring vistas. It was as if all the boredom of Sydney had been rounded up and herded into one place. Winter was cold, not the everlasting, freeze-your-socks cold of Britain but enough sometimes to whiten the ground, and summer was like an overheated oven in which tempers rose with the temperature, relieved only when the cool, gusty wind called the Southerly Buster swept across the dusty suburbs with a banging of doors and rattling of windows.

Hogan went to Parramatta Marist Brothers and then Parramatta High School, a couple of train stops from Granville. He was not a good scholar. He sat in the classrooms, looking out to where the sun was shining and wondering, for Gawd's sake, what he was doing indoors. A classmate at Marist Brothers, Phil Ruthven, said Hogan was constantly bored and would put on an act to disrupt the class. Pat Connelly remembered him as a 'cocky, independent kid. He was a bit of a loner, but not an anti-social one.' He was good at sport. He was also not bad at making a little money on the side. When crewcuts and square haircuts were in fashion, Hogan and a mate charged their friends 40 cents for a quick trim in the locker room during the lunch-hour. Hogan would take the bookings and money, and while his mate did the cutting he would keep guard, as the school did not encourage this type of private enterprise.

Hogan's problems with school – in fact, with his entire early life – may have arisen because he was a particularly intelligent person, often topping 90 per cent in English exams; but he became bored too easily. The teachers despaired of him. 'Hogan showed a rating of 140-plus in the IQ test last year,' a disillusioned teacher told his class. 'He's squandering his God-given talents. He'll live to regret it.' A figure of 140 made him close to a genius.

Hogan didn't see it that way. All he saw around him was boredom stretching forever, a life as desolate as a desert unless he did something to brighten it up. 'I got on all right at school, I just found it boring. My parents were furious. They had great hopes for me to become a lawyer. All the vocational tests

Still the 'cocky, independent kid' with an eye on the main chance.

Apart from the croc teeth in the hat, it could almost be a scene from a John Wayne western; of course, it's from *'Crocodile' Dundee*.

showed I was cut out for it. I couldn't see it myself and I still can't. Lawyers make people cry and I'm in the business of making people laugh, which is a beaut way to make a quid.'

He was at school when he first got himself into the sort of trouble that was to dog him until the day he discovered there was money in making people laugh. With his brother he tried to steal wood from a wood yard to make propellers for their bicycles, it being a well-established fact that a bike without a propeller was merely a pavement-bound machine that could not reach the stars.

The blokes had hundreds of them [bits of wood] lying around the wood yard. We just picked up a couple to put on our pushbikes and some big mug comes over and grabbed them off us and kicked us up the arse. So we went around the back of the wood yard and got all the sawdust and newspapers and piled it up against the place and set it on fire. And the bloody place caught on fire, too. Four hundred quid worth of damage. My old man had to pay for it. That was me first criminal offence. Arson!

He wasn't a movie buff but went to the Saturday matinées and Friday-night sessions at the Granville cinema, the Crest and the Castle, where he rolled circular Jaffa lollies down the aisles and talked hesitantly to the local girls. In those days cinemas were the social centres for kids too young for the pubs and clubs. His preference was for Tarzan adventures and John Wayne westerns. Many years later he ran into John Wayne in the foyer of a hotel.

'G'day,' he said, unable to think of anything else.

'Good day to you, young fella,' said Wayne, loping past.

'Stone the crows!' said an awed Hogan to himself.

At fifteen, he concluded there was more to life than school. Girls, for instance. And something in his pockets besides holes. With teachers predicting a bleak future, he became an apprentice moulder, going to technical college four nights a week to learn metallurgy. For a couple of months he stuck it out but he was not happy; it was as boring as school. Looking around for other gainful employment, he learned that the Granville Olympic Swimming Pool needed an attendant. This was more like it, more suitable for what he considered were his talents, which at that age were basically spent pursuing a good, uncomplicated time. Working at the pool meant days with the sun warm on his back and girls with whom he could flirt. This was the life.

When the pool closed for winter, he took any job he could find – working on the railways, with the water board, on the roads, labouring on building sites, anything that brought in money while he waited for the long summer to begin.

But it was a narrow existence in a bleak suburb. Australia was prosperous, the Korean War having boosted the economy; jobs were plentiful with the unemployment rate averaging a mere two per cent and inflation around three-and-a-half per cent. A lad could tell the boss to get stuffed and find a new job the next day. But under the parental gaze of the Robert Menzies government, the country was mentally asleep; it was as stimulating, though not as relaxing, as dozing on a desert island. So the western suburbs of Sydney became the spawning ground of a cult whose members were known as bodgies – kids joined together in a mateship of pegged trousers, Lurex jumpers, greased hair and an admiration for the music of Presley and Haley. They were also partial to a drop of violence, using the physical because there was nothing to spark the mental.

Hogan in a TV portrayal of Elvis, one of his childhood heroes.

Hogan soon became known to almost every cop in the area, more so when he decided to become the owner of a motorbike – an ambition of most kids in the area, that or an old bomb of a car.

I was mad on motorbikes, I had a beautiful 500 BSA Gold Star. It was a track-racin' machine and I bought it off a bloke who had worked and worked on it. It wouldn't have won any prizes for looks. It was a terrible ugly old thing but could do about 120 mph. I used to get to the traffic lights next to a Road Rocket or Thunderbird and they'd look at you with contempt. And then you'd go, you'd leave them for dead. But being a young lair, the bike was too ugly. I had to get a Triumph, all chrome work and everything. And every time you went as much as round the block the copper would pull you over. I remember once I broke about eleven traffic violations in about 600 yards. One time I was doing a handstand on the bike when, you wouldn't guess, a cop car came around the corner. They made me wheel the bike home, from Parramatta to Granville, and followed me all the way home.

In his black leather jacket with skull and crossbones painted across the back, he was a well-known figure in the area, another young but growing thorn in the side of the police, who reckoned they had better things to do than hunt young lairs. Finally an exasperated sergeant called him into the local station.

'Look, son,' he said, 'you've got fourteen traffic offences against you. I'll make a deal.'

'Like what?'

'You get rid of your bike and I'll forget them.'

'And if I don't?'

'We'll proceed. You'll lose your licence for twelve months and it'll cost you about 400 quid.'

Hogan didn't need his IQ of 140 to understand that his future would be rosier without motorbikes. He agreed.

Back at the Granville pool he developed a talent for diving; in fact he was extremely good at it, coming runner-up in both the springboard and high board in the state championships. But his make-up didn't agree with the discipline of competition diving, with one-

A bit of a tearaway in his youth, perhaps – but the adult Hogan has always contented himself with sedate pursuits such as skate-boarding.

and-halfs and backward pikes. He preferred the antics of a clown. So that's what he became – a clown diver with a troupe performing at many of the big swimming carnivals in the city. 'You could say that was the start of me showbiz career,' he joked later. 'In point of fact, that was where I first heard the roar of the crowd and whiffed the greasepaint.' But as with most things he became bored and gave it away because it was 'just the same old thing all the time'.

While he was busy impressing the girls at the pool with his fancy diving, he met his wife Noelene. She noticed him and thought, 'Who's that? He's got a big ticket on himself.' Hogan noticed her because she was 'a real water rat' and said to his mates: 'Cop that great-lookin' bird.'

They got married. Or as Hogan put it:

I was nineteen and Noelene was eighteen and the prospects were zero. To begin with I was never the wag people think I was. I wasn't the sort of bloke who got up at parties and told gags. I might get up at a party and sing if I was conned into it, but I'd rather have a fight. I had a tremendous sympathy for the underdogs. The old underdog syndrome was a bit of a hobby with me. Always stickin' me nose in where it didn't belong. Got a lot of hidings because of it. I was always going up to people and saying, 'Why don't you pick on someone your own size, you mug?' And the mug, who was always six stone heavier than me, would go bang . . . [I was] a big-mouth. I've always been aggressive. Pig-headed. Frustrated, I think, really. Frustrated with what I was doing . . .

This may have kept him, or those who watched, amused but it wasn't doing a lot for the marriage. The Hogans had three children in quick succession, money was short and Hogan decided he could earn a reasonable living by punting, a notion that has kept the bankruptcy courts occupied for years. Investing reasonable amounts to begin with, Hogan built up a nice little bank, but he dressed as if he made his living by going through garbage cans. Understandably Noelene was upset.

'Why don't you go and buy a suit?' she said in exasperation.'

'No, I'm not using this,' he said, indicating his money roll. 'It's me puntin' money, it's sacred.'

'Well, then, a pair of new shoes?'

'New shoes? I can't afford new shoes.' Then in jeans and bare feet, with £2,000 in his pocket, he would trudge to the local bookmaker, who was ever-willing to accommodate all comers. He lost the lot in two Saturdays. In one last desperate attempt to be the man who beat the bookies, he went home, scraped up all the cash he could as well as a tax cheque, and lost that too. Having failed as a punter, Hogan decided to become lightweight boxing champion of the world. He trained at a gymnasium, which happened to be the front for an illegal SP (starting price) bookmaker. In those days SP bookies were – and still are – a source of considerable annoyance to authorities. Punters were able to bet at the track or with the government-run TAB, which had offices throughout the State. But the TABs were cheerless establishments, bets had to be received well before a race and winnings were not paid until some considerable time after correct weight was declared. The SP booking took bets up to race start and paid immediately after, often at a better price than the TAB. Almost every suburban pub had a bookie, and if the law became too inquisitive, or bribe money was not being received in the right quarters, they operated from such places as gymnasiums.

Hogan, who has fond memories of the place, has described the activities at his local establishment:

Every Saturday at midday we'd go to the gym. And for five quid each we'd put on all our gear, gloves, trunks – the whole set-up – and we'd sit near the ring. And all around us everyone was puntin' like mad on the horses. There'd be anything from 70 to 150 blokes in the place. And when the coppers came, and that happened about three times, a bell would ring and me and Tiger [his boxing partner] would jump into the ring and begin beltin' the daylights out of each other. And all the punters would charge and hang over the ring and, well, Sugar Ray Robinson at the peak of his career never had a more attentive or appreciative audience. The punters would jam around the ring and never dare look away, never lettin' their eyes off us in case they caught the eye of a copper. And the coppers would walk around and see these two mugs beltin' the daylights out of each other and all the blokes jammed around the ring. They would know, of course, but there wasn't much they could do about it because it looked like a legitimate boxing session.

After a while they moved the gym out of there and set up the place as a social club. They shoved in a couple of quoit pegs and a couple of tables with cards on 'em. So when the coppers came and the bell went everyone would rush over and play quoits and cards. You'd get twenty blokes standing around intently watching a game of quoits. And there'd be blokes sitting around the card tables, some with three cards and some with eight, and yelling, 'I've got two pairs. What's trumps?'

As it turned out, Hogan was a reasonable boxer; he had no difficulty fighting his way out of a paper bag, to borrow a much used Australian expression. He had 24 bouts for 19 wins and a 'few no-contests, seeing as how sometimes I lost me cool and got disqualified'. Sometimes he would go to the Sydney Stadium, a vast sprawling tin shed known affectionately as the House of Stoush, as a stand-by fighter, picking up a few pounds each time even though he was never called on to perform. Hogan gave up the idea of being world lightweight champion when he came up against fighters who were handier and hungrier. So often was his nose broken that doctors had to remove the main bone, leaving it pliable like warm plasticine.

However, it didn't stop him using his fists on the streets, as he demonstrated when he became a union organizer. Bored with every job he had taken on, he thought he saw a future with the ironworkers' union. The officials of the union, in turn, thought he might be useful because he had the gift of the gab. He could talk the leg off an iron pot, so he was the right person to go to strike meetings and stir up those with less than militant tendencies.

But there wasn't much stirring. Mostly Hogan collected overdue union fees, of which there were many – a job he saw as little more than that of a debt collector, an occupation which ranks on the Australian social scale somewhere below that of a grave-robber. He felt it was degrading.

One day he said to a union member: 'You're twelve months behind with your union dues. 'Bout time you paid up.'

The worker shrugged. 'Why should I have

Hogan had his nose broken so often while he was a boxer that the doctors threw the bone away. Perhaps at that stage it looked something like this.

to pay the money? What did the union ever do for me?'

And so on. It was a familiar cry but Hogan was out of patience. He clipped the worker on the ear. The union decided he wasn't the right man for collecting overdue fees, Hogan found it would take more than three weeks to become national secretary, so he went looking for another job.

'Gawd, I was a larrikin,' he recalled. 'In those days I would just as soon smack someone in the ear as talk to him. I was always getting into trouble with the cops. Nothing real bad, mind – pissin' in the street, drunk and disorderly, that sort of thing . . . Always sticking me nose in where it didn't belong.'

Perhaps Hogan was too harsh on himself.

To others he was a likeable knockabout who enjoyed a few drinks, as most workers did, but nothing more than an also-ran in the outrageous stakes. Allan Buxton, who used to drink with him at the Greenacres Hotel, said: 'He's been painted as a loud-mouthed macho man, but that's bullshit. He'd go to work at 7.30, come home at 4, have a few schooners and go home to his family.'

Hogan gave up fighting when, bloodied and begrimed, he looked up from the floor of a Granville Hotel and saw his wife and children. It shook him. In his words:

I was 21 years old at the time with two kids and another on the way. I got into this fight at the pub and I knocked the fellow down the stairs. I jumped on him and we were rollin' around and I looked up and there on the footpath were me wife and kids looking at me. There I was on the ground with a mob of yobbos around me and blood everywhere and suddenly I realized I was meant to be a husband and father and not a teenage mug lout. It was so embarrassing I didn't go home for two

**With Noelene and four of the little Hogans
outside their home at Chullora.**

nights. But it changed me. I moved out of Granville about six weeks after that.

The Hogans shifted to a three-bedroom fibro NSW Housing Commission home in Chullora, not far from the sprawling railway workshops, a suburb no better and no worse than Granville. But it got Hogan away from an environment that was set to ruin him.

For a while he worked as a plant operator for the Department of Main Roads, yet another job in a long succession of jobs. The department controlled the Sydney Harbour Bridge. Sometimes he'd take messages to the vast steel structure spanning the harbour. He liked what he saw. One day the telephone rang for his boss. Hogan took it and the person on the other end asked if anyone there was interested in working as a rigger on the bridge.

'Yeah, as a matter of fact I happen to know someone,' said Hogan, remembering which end was for dancing and which for thinking. He put the telephone down, went to the bridge and applied for the job himself, not knowing, of course, that this was a decision that would ultimately change the lives of many people, not least his own. He knew only that it was about the 25th job he'd had since leaving school.

'*Hogan was a good enough fellow, a bit lazy on the job, a bit of a bludger.*'
Archie Wotherspoon

Sydney is proud of its bridge, even if after 55 years the city is still paying for it and the eight lanes of roadway are choked by traffic most of the day; a car breakdown in one lane during the morning rush can make a third of Sydney late for work. So fond are Sydneysiders of their bridge that a number have used it as a stepping stone into eternity. In the first 50 years of the bridge close to 100 people have fallen from it, most of them self-propelled. Built by the British firm Dorman Long of Middlesbrough and completed in 1932, it's a huge steel knot tying together Dawes Point on the south side of Sydney Harbour to Milson's Point on the north shore. The arch stands 135 metres above the water at high tide, the span is 503 metres long, the grey granite pylons are 87 metres high, and the total length of the bridge, including approaches, is almost 3.9 kilometres. Besides the traffic lanes, it carries a footpath and dual railway tracks.

The bridge is not a construction of notable beauty. Robin Boyd, in *The Australian Ugliness* (1960), thought the stone pylons were a useless appendage destroying the visual harmony of the steel bridge, and called them 'a triumph of disruptive patterning'. But Sydneysiders would suggest that Boyd was merely looking for an argument. They see nothing displeasing in the pylons, or for that matter in any other part of the bridge. It's a bloody good bridge. Apart from its practical function of being the quickest way across the harbour, Sydney embraces the bridge for a number of reasons, one being a fond memory of the farcical opening ceremony that took place after nine years of construction. The official ceremony was to be performed by the NSW Premier Jack Lang, but waiting in the wings, so to speak, was a certain Captain de Groot, a member of an extreme right-wing group called the New Guard.

A contemporary report in the *Sydney Morning Herald* (21 March 1932) stated:

An officer of the New Guard, Captain de Groot, caused a sensation at the official opening ceremony of the Bridge on Saturday morning, when he rode his horse up to the ribbon stretched across the highway and slashed it through with his sword.

He was taken from his horse by police officers, placed under arrest, and sent to the Reception House where he remained over the weekend. He will be charged in a closed court at the Reception House this morning with being a person deemed to be insane, and not under proper care and control.

The incident occurred just after the Premier (Mr Lang) had finished speaking, and while the Minister for Works (Mr Davidson) was on his feet. The horseman rode up to and on to the bridge behind the Governor-General's official military escort. He wore a captain's uniform, but had a cap instead of the usual cocked hat. This little difference was apparently unobserved in official quarters.

When the military escort reached Bridge Street, de Groot's horse slipped on the damp pavement and he fell some distance behind the escort. A policeman on traffic duty unwittingly assisted him to regain his place by holding up traffic to facilitate his progress . . .

The Premier's voice was carried by amplifiers to the dais where the ribbon stretched across the bridge, and, shortly after he had finished his speech, and while Mr Davidson was speaking, the man spurred his horse up to the ribbon, and with an underhand swish with his sword at the ribbon, said: 'On behalf of decent and loyal citizens of New South Wales, I now declare this bridge open.'

So Hogan reported for work on Sydney's favourite landmark. Up into the massive girders he went, up into a legend – and a fairly stiff breeze most of the time. All around lay Sydney: to the east, sleazy King's Cross, once a bohemian place of raffish charm, now a cesspit where 12-year-olds, male and female, sell their bodies on one corner for the price of a heroin deal they make on the next corner; further east, the soaring, expensive apartment blocks of Point Piper and Darling Point, some occupied by those who supply the heroin; to the south, the disposable glass towers of the Central Business District standing as testaments to the political contacts of the property developers; to the north, the colourful cubes of the advertising industry and commerce, a funhouse mirror reflection of the south; to the west, the suburbs stretching carelessly to the foot of the Blue Mountains; and beneath and beyond the harbour, 'groping across the piers and jetties, clutching deeply into the hills, the water dyed a whole paint-box armoury of colour with every breath of air, every shift of light or shade, according to the tide, the clock, the weather and the state of the moon,' as Kenneth Slessor described it in his *Portrait of Sydney*, the waters touching the soul of the city and Doyles fish and chip shop at Watson's Bay before shouldering easily through The Heads and out to sea.

Hogan liked the view and didn't mind the height. 'It's no more dangerous walking across a six-inch girder 400 feet up than six inches off the ground.'

But there were times when he wondered if he should have found employment closer to the ground, when his heart beat faster and the throat dried. These moments occurred when like all bridge workers he was confronted with someone anxious to depart this vale of tears and adhering to a fine tradition by doing it from the bridge. For one thing the headlines were always better. A person turning on the gas wouldn't rate a paragraph in the press. Someone who jumped from the bridge would make at least page 5. Hogan displayed a down-to-earth approach to would-be jumpers. When he saw one climbing the girders he would shout above the roar of the wind and the traffic: 'What d'yer think you're doing, yer silly bastard?'

Sometimes it worked. Other times it didn't. One day a man was sitting on the edge of a pylon mentally preparing himself for the last act of his life. Hogan strolled over to him, lit a cigarette – it was part of the act, a kind of reassurance of normality – and asked him what in Gawd's name was he doing.

'I'm going to jump, I'm going to jump,' the man screamed.

Hogan stretched out a hand. 'No, you're not, you silly bastard. Come here and stop being ridiculous.'

Back in the old routine on Sydney Harbour Bridge: heights were never any problem for Hogan, though would-be suicides occasionally were.

And the man threw himself into space, splattering on the concrete below.

On another occasion Hogan and a group of workmates were sitting in a crane when they saw a man, heavily built, about 22 years old, climbing up the arch towards them.

'Here's comes a jumper,' someone said. Experienced in these matters, they could tell a would-be suicide not only from the single-minded way he moved but from the obvious fact that he shouldn't have been there in the first place.

'All right,' said Hogan, 'when he gets to us I'll get out and stop him. The rest of you jump him when I give the nod.'

They agreed it was a satisfactory arrangement. No one wanted to be the volunteer who actually tackled the man. When the jumper came closer, Hogan remembered the old army dictum about never volunteering, because the man was much bigger than he had originally assumed, built like a brick wall with a verandah for shoulders.

Standing in front of him, Hogan demanded: 'Where do you think you're going?'

'Get out of my way,' the man grunted.

Hogan turned to his workmates for help, but they too had noted the man's size and quickly found other matters with which to occupy themselves. They weren't about to wrestle with a brick wall on a narrow girder high above the harbour.

The man brushed past Hogan as if he wasn't there. This annoyed Hogan, who thought, 'Bugger you, you're not going to push me aside like that. You're not beating me, son.' So he went after him, grabbing him with one hand and holding on to a steel railing with the other. The man heaved, Hogan held, his hand gripping the railing so hard he thought he would leave finger marks on the steel.

'Let me go,' the man shouted. Hogan began talking. He chattered about this and that, but mostly he spoke on the disadvantages of jumping into space and becoming another bridge statistic. After a while the man agreed there were better things to do and followed Hogan down the arch.

About halfway down the man suddenly turned, picked up Hogan as if he were a feather and screamed: 'I could throw you over, you know.'

Keeping as calm as he could – not easy considering the circumstances – Hogan agreed. 'Yeah, I know you could, but why should you want to do that? I haven't done anything to hurt you.'

Thinking about it for a while, the man could find no valid reason why Hogan should be tossed from the bridge; instead he followed him down. But when he was grabbed by waiting police he went berserk, tossing around

A former workmate claims that at one time 90 per cent of the Bridge's rigging came out of Hogan's head.

Hogan, who was holding on to one leg, like a rag doll. After he was put into a straitjacket, the man asked for a glass of water. When it was handed to him he bit a chunk out of the glass, then the finger of a policeman who tried to remove the glass from his mouth.

Hogan recalled: 'He was a uni student and working part-time as well, on uppers and downers to keep going, and he was just coming down off a bad trip. Only 22 and he wanted to end it all.' Hogan received a Royal Humane Society medal for the rescue.

Hogan was a good rigger, innovative, often coming up with new ways to do things. Athol Gilmore, one of his workmates, comments:

He's very accomplished in any field he'd like to try. On the Harbour Bridge I'd say practically 90 per cent of the rigging that's down there now all came out of his head. They were doing things the same way as they did in 1930 and he said to me, 'God Almighty, Gilly, we're doing this the hard way.' He'd think of something else that was easier and quicker and better all round.

Sometimes Hogan and Gilmore would stroll through the city for what they called their galah-watching expeditions, that is observing anyone showing off or skiting. Hogan wasn't to know it then but he was already collecting the characters that he would later transfer to television.

Dog men – the blokes who ride a load to the tops of high buildings – were among the champions. Riggers. Blokes on construction sites. That was me entertainment. I never went looking at the strange things people do – watchin' a bloke trying to pick up a bird or watchin' the butcher trying to get rid of the fat lady and serve the good sort – I didn't do that as research. It was me street theatre, pure and simple.

One dogman would take a load up on the crane and every time some pretty girl went by he'd lean out that little bit further, singing out loud to the driver up above. He was really bungin' on an act to make himself look daring. Yet as soon as the girl had gone he'd just stand on the load and look real daggy. It cracked me up for about five minutes. You get the same sort of posers at parties trying to impress people. And on buses. The conductor will come to a pretty girl passenger, the old cap will get tilted to the back of the head and his whole manner becomes more dashing.

Working on the Bridge provided ample opportunity for studying posers – and there was to be a memorable succession of these in later years on *The Paul Hogan Show*.

Although he made a few good mates on the bridge, some considered him big-headed, abrasive, too much of a loner. And some thought he had a strange sense of humour. Athol Gilmore recalls: 'He wasn't popular with all the guys. He was too straightforward and honest. There's a lot of the Robin Hood in him. Standing up for the little fellow and the bloke that wasn't doing so good. But he was a joy to work with. He was funny, and he was funny all the time.'

Another workmate, Derek Quinn, comments: 'Up here on the bridge he'd crack a smark-aleck remark about somebody and they'd come back at him and he'd immediately come back with an answer. Half the people he made fun of [later] actually worked here. In his early shows his characters all came from here.'

Archie Wotherspoon remembers him as 'a good enough fellow, a bit lazy on the job, a bit of a bludger. He was pretty selfish at times and he always got what he wanted.'

However, whatever it was Hogan wanted he was not finding it on the bridge. He kept telling himself there had to be more to life than getting up early in the morning to work in sometimes atrocious conditions on a dangerous job, having a few beers then going home. And sometimes getting into trouble.

I didn't know then what I wanted. I just knew I

Pictured in 1982. If he hadn't been bored out of his brain by his job on 'the coat-hanger', Hogan might never have made the change to show business.

didn't want to get up at 6.30 in the morning and go trudgin' off and crawlin' around the Harbour Bridge. I was frustrated. Working to eat and just bored out of me brain by the job. If you're stuck in a job like that try and get out. The most important thing if you work for a livin' is to enjoy your bloody work, because you spend a third of your life at it. You're better off getting a few bucks less at your job and bein' happy at it . . . I've never been interested in being five feet ahead. I'd like to be a hundred yards ahead.

He left the bridge for other jobs a couple of times but came back, still searching.

In those days a television show called *New Faces* enjoyed high ratings. Basically a talent quest, its popularity lay in the cruel comments the judges would make to the contestants, sometimes ridiculing them to the point of tears. The humiliation both repulsed and attracted viewers and the show was the most discussed television event of the early 'seventies. Hogan reckoned it was like Christians, played by contestants, being fed to the lions, or judges. During their morning tea-break the riggers would discuss the previous night's performances.

'I can do better than that mug,' Hogan would say.

'So why don't you have a go?' his workmates would reply.

'Just might at that.'

'Yeah, and pigs might fly.'

Young Hogan – not afraid to risk public humiliation on the TV show *New Faces* in order to make a show-business breakthrough.

He would say much the same thing at home as he watched the show, finding little amusement in comedians who began: 'Now, take my wife . . . Will somebody *please* take her?' To anyone within earshot he compared his abilities as a bar-room comic to those he had seen on *New Faces*. 'Look, at them, they're all Pommies. Can't someone get up there and be an Australian? Gawd, if I couldn't do better than that I'd give up.'

'If you think you can, why don't you go and do it?' said Noelene patiently.

Finally his bluff was called. He had to put up or shut up. Inexplicably there was a long wait to get on to *New Faces*. Numerous people were willing to sacrifice themselves on the altar of humiliation in the chance, however remote, of breaking into show business. Hogan didn't have the patience to wait. Putting some thought into it, he wrote to the programme claiming to have been an acrobat in a circus, a sheep-shearer, a collector of night soil and that he came from Lightning Ridge (the only truthful line in his letter). He said he performed as a knife-throwing tap-dancer.

'That'll get 'em in,' he said to Noelene.

It did. Hogan was accepted ahead of others. As he went to the television studios, he thought, 'If I'm going to make a mug of myself

Filming on the Bridge, years after leaving his job as a rigger, for an American tourism commercial.

I'll be a real mug and cure myself for all time.'

Hogan strolled in front of the cameras wearing shorts, singlet and gumboots and carrying a plastic garbage bin and three home-made wooden knives. The judges blinked. They would have blinked more had they known that by now he had worked up such an intense dislike for them that he was thinking of causing them physical damage if their remarks were too insulting. Splendid television, no doubt, but an attitude that did not guarantee much of a future.

His attitude was not improved by the way the act before him was treated. A young girl, a jazz dancer, was gonged off the show after 30 seconds, and Hogan, concerned as usual for the underdog, thought, 'You lousy bastards, you better not do that to me.'

As it happened, the judges realized they were being treated to a refreshingly new type of humour, however raw. They watched Hogan send up a few bad television commercials then do a tap dance in gumboots before announcing his speciality, which was throwing knives while blindfolded. He didn't have a blindfold, so he put the garbage bin on his head instead.

Scoring top marks for the night, he was invited to go on a bigger version of the show which went to Melbourne as well as Sydney.

only in Sydney, the Melbourne judges not having a clue what he was talking about.

'That's the end of me show-business career,' he told Noelene.

And so it would have been but for Desmond Tester, producer of *New Faces*. He saw Hogan as a chunk of raw talent that needed cutting and polishing, like the opals dug from the hard rock of Lightning Ridge, before being presented to the public again. Hogan reappeared as Australia's first one-man band without instruments, again an excuse to talk. The next year he was invited back and he appeared as a thunderbox player (thunderbox is an old slang name for an outside toilet). Hogan explains:

I ordered two tea-chests from the studio, which they provided, but they wanted me to rehearse first. I said I couldn't, it was too dangerous and anyway I could only play the thunderbox once. They said no one goes on without rehearsing. We had a real argument and they weren't going to put me in but I managed to convince them. When they saw me act they realized why I couldn't rehearse. You see I did a bit of a spiel and a tap dance and then said I'd play the thunderbox. And what I did was run across the stage and crash me skull through the tea-chests. I claimed it hit an A note.

This unusual demonstration of the wit and wisdom of the ocker at large got Hogan into the grand finals. The instrument he chose this time was the garbophone, another creation that would have pleased Gerald Hoffnung. The garbophone consisted of a tin flute inside a plastic garbage bin played at the same time as the bin was pushed in and out like an accordion. For the rest of his act he abused the judges, telling them in their own clichés what they were doing wrong: the Christians biting the lions, as he later put it.

'When you play the mouth organ you should smile a little bit,' he said acidly.

Beaten to first place by a 15-year-old cello player, Hogan believed once more that he had reached the end of his show-business career, such as it had been. He took it philosophically because, after all, he had only gone on 'for a lark'.

He went back to the Harbour Bridge. But he had not gone unnoticed in the television industry. His ten years of working as a rigger were about to end.

Scoring a winner in 1973. 'A chunk of raw talent that needed cutting and polishing' was how the *New Faces* producer saw Hogan.

This time he was presented as a shovel player, although it was merely an excuse for him to do what he wanted and what he did best – talk at length and kick the stuffing out of bad commercials, of which there were many on Sydney television. The shovel act came at the end, when he banged two shovels together as the band played. But he went over like the proverbial lead balloon because he didn't know the commercials he had sent up were screened

In a small, ugly cottage in the Sydney suburb of Willoughby, close by the studios, offices and transmission towers of TCN9, Michael Willesee looked at ways to improve his television programme, a half-hour current affairs show screening five nights a week and called, simply, *A Current Affair*. Although the programme was moderately successful, Willesee, head of Transmedia, the packaging company, and anchorman of the programme, believed some humour was necessary, and it could be best achieved by having an ocker figure commenting on the day's news, in much the same fashion as a newspaper cartoonist. But Willesee was finding that entertaining ockers were in short supply. Ockers who could fart and belch and drop their trousers were plentiful. There was no shortage of ockers who could sing bawdy songs and abuse Poms and chunder on cue. But there seemed to be none who, while retaining their larrikin Australian character, could raise a laugh without being gross. After all, he didn't want to bring the public bar near closing time into the lounge of decent folk. He had written scripts and auditioned actors but none was right for the rôle.

One day, in 1971, a reporter for the programme, Tony Ward, approached Willesee. 'That character you've been looking for, well, I saw a bloke on *New Faces* the other night. He could be the right one.'

'What's he do?'

'Works on the bridge.'

'On the bridge? That's a good start. We'll get a tape of him and have a look.'

After seeing a tape of Hogan's *New Faces* performance, Willesee agreed with Ward. The man had possibilities. He was raw but he was original.

'Tell you what,' he said to Ward. 'We won't audition him. You go to the Harbour Bridge and interview him under the guise of congratulating him for coming second in *New Faces*. We'll see how he copes.'

Hogan coped extremely well. Tony Ward had previously been the star of an Australian-made series called *Hunter* in which he played a government agent in pursuit of criminals and spies and anyone else liable to sully the fair land.

When the camera started rolling on the bridge, Hogan took the initiative from Ward. 'You were Hunter once, weren't you?' he said, poking Ward's stomach. 'You have it too soft now, sittin' in a big chair instead of chasin' crooks around the country. Time we got you into condition.'

The next moment he had Ward puffing away at a series of push-ups on the metal floor of the bridge, then, with one foot on Ward's back, pumping up and down, launched into an amusing monologue on the dubious joys of working on the bridge. Back at the cottage where *A Current Affair* was produced, Willesee, after seeing the segment, was convinced Hogan was the right person to play the ocker. He invited Hogan in for a filmed interview. It went well, with Hogan ad-libbing and Willesee unable to control his mirth.

'What I liked,' Willesee said to Hogan, 'was the pace of the interview.'

'My bloody oath it had pace,' said Hogan. 'I saw a train comin' across the bridge and I reckoned we had two minutes to do the interview before we couldn't hear a thing.'

In the backyard of the cottage, Hogan auditioned with a camera crew. Willesee knew he was on the right track when the crew laughed; in fact laughter from the camera crew became the gauge of the acceptability of Hogan's segments in the following months. If its members didn't laugh Hogan rewrote his scripts, usually in a few minutes on scraps of paper, until he got them chuckling.

Hogan was not used every night, only when there was something that lent itself to his style of humour. He continued on the bridge but now he was a personality. His workmates were not short on suggestions and Hogan listened to their ideas and watched their mannerisms. But not too closely. 'When you're up 400 feet you've gotta think about what you're doing. If you think about television you end up on the road, scrambled.'

Willesee found it increasingly difficult to work with someone not immediately at hand. For instance, when he needed him, Willesee would ring the bridge asking for Hogan. 'Sure, just hang on a minute,' the person who answered would say, and 20 minutes would pass before Hogan could be found somewhere on the bridge. Surveys showed that Hogan was rapidly becoming popular, the cartoon figure that had long been sought, but he was not much good to Willesee up on the bridge. There was no choice but to make Hogan an offer to join the show on a full-time basis.

'We haven't got much money,' he explained to Hogan. 'I can give you 90 bucks a week. But you better think about it because most people fail in this business. And it's not all glamour. Talk it over with Noelene.'

Hogan thought it over for about five seconds. 'I can handle it.'

'You sure?'

'No worries.'

So for the last time Hogan left the bridge, and without regrets. The response to his television appearances was extraordinary. Viewers either loved him or hated him; among the latter was Clyde Packer, son of Sir Frank and brother of Kerry, who was then in charge of TCN9. He told Willesee to get rid of Hogan because of the large number of viewers who had rung to complain about his ocker presence.

It took Hogan roughly five seconds to decide whether to quit his job as a rigger.

'I can't do that,' Willesee said.

'Why not, indeed?'

'Well, when we walk down the street to buy hamburgers for lunch and everyone's calling out to him and not me, I know it's working.'

What also convinced Willesee was a recently published public opinion poll on the popularity and non-popularity of well-known individuals. Hogan came third in the rankings of the most popular television personality and first in the most unpopular. It was exactly the reaction Willesee wanted.

Another survey, this time among 4,000 schoolchildren, showed that 21 per cent thought he was the best single component of the show, as against seven per cent for his boss, the urbane, professional Willesee. Other surveys showed that women liked him because of his weatherbeaten good looks, fair hair and blue eyes, men because he seemed the sort of good fellow with whom they would like to share a drink after work or around a keg at a backyard barbecue.

With John Cornell as 'Strop' (right), wearing the customary silly hat, and Michael Willesee (centre) in 1973.

His segments, lasting two or three minutes, were often produced in the backyard of Willesee's bungalow. Hogan would write his script on scraps of paper, usually taking no more than half an hour. Other times he would go in cold and ad lib. Somehow it worked.

The television critics, myself included, generally agreed he was appalling, and should return to the bridge or Lightning Ridge – anywhere, as long as he wasn't in front of the cameras. At that time I wrote a weekly television column for the Sydney *Daily Mirror* under the byline Veritas. The brief given Veritas was to write 'without fear or favour', in other words, to lay into television programmes as hard as possible within the laws of libel. The name of the person writing Veritas was supposed to be a secret so sacred it could be extracted only under pain of torture on the

rack, or perhaps with a couple of beers, and when he appeared in public – on television panels, for example, discussing this and that – he wore a hood like those of professional wrestlers who enter the ring under such names as the 'Masked Madman'. Actually I was but one in a long line of journalists who were Veritas, the name and tradition passed along in much the same fashion as those of the comic-book character 'The Phantom'. It was a tolerably amusing gimmick and quite successful. And so, keeping to tradition, I attacked Hogan under the heading: 'Get This Ugly Australian Off Television.'

Hogan was furious. 'Who is this galah?' he asked Willesee. 'I reckon I should go round and hang one on him.'

Willesee calmed him down. 'It's the greatest publicity you could ever get,' he said.

'Yeah, but why should I have to put up with it?'

'It's a part of the game.'

'Tell you what, if anyone said that to me

When Hoges first became famous on TV, there were many critics who thought that as a comedian he'd make a good rigger.

when I was on the bridge, he would have been biffed.'

Other critics were no kinder. One wrote: 'I watch your performances . . . with my eyebrows arched in derision and my jaw cracking with boredom.' Said another: 'To present Hogan as an original wit is to stretch a flimsy talent altogether too far.'

Since then Hogan has had little time for critics, being in full accord with Cecil B. DeMille, who once said he made pictures for people, not critics. About eighteen months after his introduction to television he said:

The only publicity I ever got in the first twelve months was a baggin'. I thought it was a bit rough. I didn't get hurt, just indignant. Being hurt is for big sheilas. I've learned my lesson. I don't take any notice of the critics, don't even bother to read them. The last time I read one he said I wasn't any

Bob Hope, for which I'm very grateful. Who wants to be a Bob Hope, standing in front of the cameras reading other people's jokes from a bit of paper? I don't mind being called rotten, boring, repetitious, vulgar, ignorant, but I do mind the misinformed clots that say very condescendingly, 'All he needs is a scriptwriter.' I'd love to have a scriptwriter if I could find one who didn't take three weeks to write a three-minute sketch. Then some prawn suggested I should have acting lessons. If I had acting lessons I'd be in *Dad and Dave* [an old radio show], not me own show.

The viewers, or at least a great number of them, sensibly ignored the critics and followed Hogan's every move. He had become their voice. In his ocker way, he was able to articulate what they thought about subjects ranging from politics to pollution. In a few months he had become so much a part of their lives that some were unable to see the joke and believed everything he said. On one occasion he suggested that if people donated $10 to the Taxation Department's Christmas party they would get their tax rebate back in a hurry. Many did just that. An embarrassed Taxation Department reported that about 1100 taxpayers took Hogan's advice, pinning $10 notes to their tax returns. 'Cripes,' said Hogan, 'I reckon after that I'll be the last person in Australia to get my rebate.'

Hogan soon learned that humour was the best defence against the barbs of critics and members of the public who thought that as a comedian he would make a good rigger. In the national magazine *TV Week* he wrote in 1972:

I can't understand these jokers who hate me. They oughta wake up to themselves. I can figure these blokes who just don't like me. There's a few jokers around this joint I don't like myself. There's those Poms who're always whingeing, see, and there's Mike Willesee always changing his mind about what he wants to do.

But I can't figure why any joker would plain hate me. Some bloke wrote in and said I was a bigot. I thought I was a bit hot with the sheilas, too, until Willesee told me it didn't mean that at all. Then Willesee told me that blokes were reckoning that I was a bigot because I called the Pommies twits. Of course not all Pommies are twits. There's got to be some good ones around.

Then a couple of sheilas wrote in saying I looked scruffy and I told Willesee he'd better cough up so I could buy some clobber. He didn't. Then a couple of blokes started saying I wasn't a reporter's you-know-what and that got me because the nongs were so stupid they didn't realize I was just having a sling – that I'm not really a reporter – just a joker who used to tighten nuts on the coat-hanger [Harbour Bridge] to stop it falling into the water. Yeah, just a nut-and-bolt tightener who went on *New Faces* once because I got sick and tired of watching those alecs who called themselves comedians getting up there on the box making idiots of themselves.

So I said to the missus one day: 'Jeez, I could do better than that.' You know what sheilas are. She went up the wall. She reckoned I'd make a fool of her. Well, I got up on the show, see, and I did pretty good. The next thing I know I'm getting a ring from this Willesee bloke to come in and do a bit on his show. Then the whole thing takes off. Sheilas are stopping me in the street and asking for the old moniker and wanting to know whether I'm hitched. When I tell them I've got four kids they don't seem interested any more. Funny about that.

When I go to the rubbity [pub] for a pot there's always some bloke who wants to know whether I'm fair dinkum. No, I tell them I'm Billy McMahon [a former prime minister] and then they reckon I'm a card. People started writing into Willesee and saying I was ruining the programme and he said: 'Well, let's give them a run for their money. Let's have a vote to see whether you should stay on the show.'

I didn't go for that one much and I told him because I could suddenly see myself without a meal ticket. 'Quit worrying,' he says, 'I know what the verdict will be now.' Well, we had the vote and I romped in by the length of the straight. Now Willesee is stuck with me. But some of the things people said about me in their votes, you'd have thought I was Billy Snedden [Federal Treasurer] after a crook budget. 'Australians don't speak like that any more,' was what most of the pie-eaters said, or 'Aussies don't carry on that way' or 'He's a disgrace to good Australians.'

What I said to Willesee about that load of garbage would have made a bullocky [bullock team driver] take his hat off to me. Those nongs couldn't see I was doing it for a giggle. Of course all Aussies don't talk like that – just most of them. Go to the footie any weekend arvo [afternoon] or to the boozer and listen a bit. You'll hear jokers like me everywhere.

Of course, I'm not really that dumb meself, see. I'm a bit smarter than I make out on the old telly . . . I'm just trying to give a few people a laugh by sending meself up and they take it serious-like. I

Always 'a bit hot with the sheilas': pictured with Linda Kozlowski, his co-star from *'Crocodile' Dundee*.

reckon I'm pretty funny. But the missus reckons I'm about as funny as a parking bluey. She says this job on the telly has been good for me, though. Shocking temper I had before. I used to blow the old stack all the time. Now I hardly ever do it. Must be because I'm contented or something.

Who wouldn't be? I'm on what Willesee calls a retainer or something and I sit at home spine-bashing waiting for the telephone to ring each morning. Sometimes Willesee wants me to do what he calls 'a piece'. 'Get down to Bondi in half an hour and do a bit on pollution,' he yells. So I hops in the car and I think what I'm going to say as I'm going along, which ain't real hard because what I don't know about pollution would fill the Opera House on opening night. Then I just spout it all off in one take at Bondi or wherever and hop in the car and go home for some more spine-bashing and a jug at the rubbity.

Yeah, this job'll do me. Better than being up

there on the old coat-hanger in the cold and the wind and hanging on by your tats [teeth] . . .

Of course, this was not Paul Hogan speaking. This was Hoges, the character Hogan invented, a pub philosopher dressed in singlet, shorts, football socks and boots, the clothing of a man doing hard manual work in the heat of a Sydney summer. Hogan is a quieter person, withdrawn at times, not a heavy drinker nor a loud mouth. Over the years Hogan has patiently explained the difference, but there are many who still refuse to acknowledge they are not one and the same, any more than Charlie Chaplin was the Little Tramp:

If I were really Hoges maybe I would be a has-been. Y'know, it gets me sometimes that there's still professional people around, especially in the press, who think that I'm the character I made. But let's face it, if I were I'd be dead already. Hoges would have come off the bridge, spent all his money on grog, tried to teach everyone how to run things, and gone out on his ear – and back to the

75

bridge. I wouldn't mind being Hoges, dazzling everyone with my instant stupidity. Look at the life he's got. He's got the game sewn up with his chook raffles and get-rich schemes. Hoges has the answer to everything. In many ways Hoges is very much me. Most comic characters are created by a script-writer and played by an actor. Alf Garnett, for instance, has no relation to Warren Mitchell, the actor. They're miles apart. But me and Hoges are very close. I just play myself – but I send myself up along with everyone else. He's sort of a character based on reality.

Perhaps Peter Faiman, director of 'Croco-dile' Dundee, put it best: 'What Hoges relates is the spirit and feelings that Paul Hogan has.'

As Hogan grew more popular by the day, Michael Willesee said to him: 'I believe you should have a manager.'

'A manager?' The idea had never crossed Hogan's mind.

'You've been getting all sorts of offers. You need someone to look after them.'

'Any suggestions?'

Enter John Cornell. To discuss Hogan without Cornell is to mention Laurel without Hardy, Abbott without Costello, Morecambe without Wise, Ronald without Nancy. Cornell was the Melbourne producer of A Current Affair and saw in Hogan an original talent that could go far beyond portraying an ocker. Cornell came from Western Australia, from a gold-mining town called Kalgoorlie ('It's my favourite town, because it's got the only legal-ized brothel in Australia and because it's a rough, honest and real Aussie place.') He became a newspaper reporter, was London editor of West Australian Newspapers, then joined Willesee's Transmedia organization as Melbourne producer of A Current Affair. Cor-nell was a self-confessed larrikin and he had that in common with Hogan. He decided to look after Hogan, even though there was no money involved at that stage. They shook hands on the deal, the only contract they have to this day. 'John's me best mate,' says Hogan simply.

Hoges/Hogan – it's often difficult to know where the Hoges character ends and the real Hogan begins. As Peter Faiman commented: 'What Hoges relates is the spirit and feelings that Paul Hogan has.'

Cornell soon had to sort out the offers coming in to Hogan to judge beauty contests and pet shows, open department stores and speak at meetings and conferences, including some at the universities of New South Wales and Victoria, invitations that amused Hogan when he recalled he left school at fifteen. At functions he could be relied upon to generate a chuckle or two, even those functions where laughs might generally be considered thin on the ground. For instance, he opened the new Comet Overnight Transport terminal in Mel-bourne in front of an audience of leaders of industry and commerce. He didn't know what they expected but what they got was a poem:

When life is pretty miserable and everything looks
black,
When your love-life runs real sour and you haven't
got a zack,
Don't let it get on top of you when you have rotten
luck,
Just come down to the Comet depot and throw
yourself under a truck.

Hogan's popularity grew so quickly that in a short time he was, to borrow a show-business cliché, a prisoner of his own success. In little more than a year he was so well known he could no longer go to a corner pub for a peaceful drink. The easy-going days when he was a rigger were rapidly becoming a memory. The public now owned him.

One afternoon we met for a couple of beers. We had been at the bar only two or three minutes when the first of a line of yobbos advanced towards us, grinning like a Hallowe-'en pumpkin, the right thumb rampant in the she's-right-mate position.

'Don't worry, mate,' said Hogan. 'I'll look after him. No one knows more about Freds [about yobbos] than me. I've been one all me life.'

The man screwed his face into a vaudeville wink, said, 'Any 'ow,' giggled, then, changing tack, floated in the direction of the men's lavatory.

'They're not so bad going into the dunny as comin' out,' explained Hogan. 'Comin' out they've got more time.'

People kept coming forward – an attacking army of admirers, thrusting into his hand

Hogan with John Cornell, his 'best mate'.

scraps of paper, notebooks, used envelopes, department-store dockets, old betting tickets, anything they could find as an instant autograph album. Hogan signed them with unfailing good humour, sometimes scratching his head or tugging an earlobe at the wonder of it all. He recalled an incident a few weeks earlier when he had appeared at the annual show or fair at Toowoomba, a country town in Queensland. He was required to stand on a dais in the hot sun and amuse the gathered townsfolk and their country cousins with the odd rib-tickler or two.

All the time I'm talking, kids are pokin' me with autograph books saying, 'Sign mine, sign mine,' and sweat is runnin' down out of me eyes and droppin' all over the place. I say to the sales manager of a television station who is with me to get the crowd back. I can't push them away myself because it's not on to hit a fan over the earhole. But he comes up like a great prawn and tells the crowd that I'm a nice bloke, which, of course, does nothing at all.

Around this time I feel a little jab in me leg. I've got me shorts on, you understand. I look down and this teenybopper has yanked out a hair on me leg. Her friends all have a little squabble over it and then someone pulls out another, and another. I'm beginnin' to feel like a bloody plucked chook. So I says to the sales manager, 'Get me off, you bloody prawn.' He finally drags me off there and people get knocked over and trampled. But all the time this is going on I'm thinking, 'Jesus Christ, what's happening? I'll just check myself over to see if I'm Elvis Presley or something.' But I'm not. I'm Hogan. A scruffy 33-year-old comic.

Hogan in one of his rock-star rôles – but he can't understand the rock-star levels of adulation he gets from women.

It was Hogan's first experience with that strange chemistry that turns nice, polite people into a ranting mob when confronted by a television personality. Hogan soon learned skilful ways to avoid the mob but was sometimes forced to spend uncomfortable hours hiding in such demeaning places as the back of a van. His appeal was spread across all strata of society and all ages. He recalled another incident a few months earlier when he appeared at a pop festival at Sunbury, near Melbourne – not as a singer, because his singing voice could best be described as rough, but as Hoges:

I couldn't believe it, 30,000 kids out there all laughin' at anything I said. And I was the cleanest bloke on stage. Like, pop groups would come and say, 'Hey, you fuckwits' and similar words, every crude thing you could think of. I would come out and say 'dunny' and they would roar laughing. I just had to say, 'I know what you're up to, smokin' grass and carrying on,' and they would think it was great.

And then on the Sunday night it happened, the sort of thing an entertainer will see only once in his lifetime and die happy. The bloke introducin' me said, 'If you want to see Hogan, you better let him know you welcome him. What about lighting up a match?' And they did! Everyone! The whole 30,000! The place was lit up like a magnificent Christmas tree. And I came out and said, 'G'day,' and I didn't have to say anything else for three minutes.

A topless girl from the audience suddenly appeared on stage, such exhibitions then being in vogue at pop festivals. Hogan handled it well. With an innocent look, he appealed to the father of 'this poor little boy' to come forward and claim 'him'. He suggested the father should 'form a queue' at one side of the stage. The crowd howled with laughter.

I asked him what he thought was the reason for his popularity. He shrugged. 'Honestly, mate, I don't know. I'm just being meself.'

By now he had got an act together with Irish singer Tim Connor, doing the rounds of pubs and clubs. He enjoyed the rough and tumble of the circuit, exchanging insults with the

With Irish singer Tim Connor, with whom Hogan did an act involving a garbage bin, in a show which they took round Australian clubs and pubs in 1973.

drunks and ocker asides with the ockers. 'One night a manager apologized because a load of ockers were causing trouble. But it didn't worry me because they turned out to be a tremendous audience. I'm much happier with people like that, who used to be me own mates, than the set in dinner suits. I suppose at heart I'm still one of 'em, despite the fact I'm richer now.'

I went with Hogan and Connor to the Oceanic Hotel at Coogee, Sydney, the entertainment lounge of which is an enormous, rambling room with a hard-drinking audience capable of killing an act in one second flat. Hogan was unhappy that the only way to the stage was through the audience, most of whom, as it was 9.30 at night, had been drinking solidly for at least two hours. Parking his car at the rear of the hotel, Hogan rummaged through a suitcase and with a flourish produced a black wig, a black moustache and an enormous pair of sunglasses only slightly smaller than a department-store window. He put them on and grinned. 'A real spiv, ain't I? No one's going to recognize me now.'

No sooner had he stepped from the car than three girls passing by whistled and shouted: 'How yer going, Hoges?'

He pretended not to hear. And then, with Connor carrying a large plastic rubbish bin, they walked through the packed lounge to the stage. Surprisingly, no one noticed them, which may have had more to do with the power of the booze on the audience than on its powers of observation.

Connor warmed up the show, introducing Hogan with a few lines stolen from 'The Wild Colonial Boy', a favourite song of tipplers.

There was a wild colonial boy,
Paul Hogan was his name
He was born and bred in Lightning Ridge . . .

The rest of the song, if indeed there were more lines, was lost in a roar of approval as Hogan walked on, clad in sleeveless shirt, shorts, football socks and boots, carrying the plastic garbage bin. ' 'Ullo there, viewers,' he shouted. 'If youse just shut your gobs youse might learn somethin'.'

He poured scorn on politicians. He extolled his virtues as a great lover, claiming that

Germaine Greer was so inhibited before she met him that she used to wear two bras. He discussed dunnies, a favourite subject with Australian comedians. Why this should be so has never been satisfactorily explained except that the word itself has an amusing ring. Dunny! It would make a wowser smile. Within seconds Hogan could do no wrong, and if he had just stood there wiggling his ears he would have had the audience in stitches.

After the performance we went to the office of the hotel manager, who was smiling as if he had won the lottery. 'Tell you something, Paul,' he said, 'I've been here twelve years and you're only the second comedian who's gone over.'

When Hogan was performing it was noticeable that many women in the audience, while laughing along with his lines, eyed him in a way that suggested they would like to know him better – much, much better. I put it to Hogan that he was rapidly developing into a sex symbol. He thought the idea preposterous. 'That's a joke, mate. Sure, you get some birds comin' up to you and putting offers to you. But there's not nearly as many as a lot of people would like to make out. Most of them just want to talk to you.'

He mentioned the name of a well-known Australian entertainer with a reputation as a Lothario.

I read about him in television magazines and everywhere he goes they reckon he's mobbed by thousands of women all tryin' to get him into the cot. Well, I arrived at a television reception and he was just in front of me. And there was just two rough, homely little birds standin' there and as he walked past they said, 'G'day, poof.' No, you could come to grief if you were a fat, ugly little slob and suddenly you're made a star and had women chasing after you. But if you'd had your fair share before you got into the business, you'd realize it was just the magic of the box . . . that it wasn't really you at all.

Years later, when promoting 'Crocodile' Dundee in the United States, he was asked much the same thing. He still thought it ridiculous that he, Hogan, a knockabout, a middle-aged father of four, could be regarded as a sex symbol, but he didn't want to be rude because the movie had to be promoted. So he turned the question round and delivered a lecture on the differences between Australian and American males and why male chauvinism is good for women but not so smart for men.

Australian men are chauvinist but, as any smart woman knows, that allows her to rule the world. Take a woman drivin' along the road as a simple example. She gets a flat tyre and what does she do, she gets out of the car and goes 'Yooo-hooo' and a man comes along and says, 'I'll fix that for you', and the stupid man gets dirty and skin off his knuckles and he fixes it up while she stands there smokin' a cigarettte and then she says, 'I couldn't have done it without you', and he beams, feels great and goes, 'Yoooooo.'

At that point Hogan let out a Tarzan holler, then went on: 'And that is how the system works. The women have the brains and the men have the brawn and I don't know what the problem is.' By then the interviewer had forgotten the question and was more than satisfied with Hogan's answer, which after all is what interviews are all about.

Not long after he was an established personality on *A Current Affair*, but was still working on the bridge, Hogan began receiving offers from perceptive advertising executives who saw him as the perfect salesman. One was to do commercials and was worth $8,000, more money than Hogan had ever had in his life.

'No, no, wait,' said Cornell. 'There'll be a better offer.'

'Wait? For how long? Till I die of old age?' Hogan complained, but decided Cornell knew better.

He was right. Already in the office of an advertising agency an offer was being mapped out that would change Hogan from an ocker comic to the hottest show-business property in Australia.

'*Poms are possibly me favourite foreigners 'cos they do try to speak English pretty good.*'
Paul Hogan

In the middle of 1972 the tobacco company Rothman's of Pall Mall (Aust.) Ltd, after considerable market research, decided to launch a new brand of cigarette. One reason was that its main rivals, British Tobacco and Phillip Morris, held eight of the top-selling brands. The other was that the Australian Labour Party under Gough Whitlam – those hard-nosed utopians, as satirist Barry Humphries called them – had declared it would ban cigarette advertising on television and radio when it became the Federal Government, and public opinion polls were indicating that this would be sooner rather than later. The new fag had to reach the market in a hurry. This occurred, of course, in the days before smoking was bad for you and you weren't made to feel like a criminal for lighting up.

Rothman's executives were especially interested in making a hole in the sales of the Benson & Hedges and Stuyvesant brands, sold on jet-setting snob appeal; if you smoked such a brand you would miraculously find yourself in Monte Carlo flicking a cigarette lighter for Princess Grace or on the polished deck of a yacht discussing the stock market with other rich layabouts. Reg Watson, Rothman's man-

For one of his Winfield cigarette commercials Hogan was a concert pianist, ably supported by the Sydney Symphony Orchestra.

aging director, wanted an Australian cigarette, not one that was international, not a 'passport to smoking pleasure', or one for 'when only the best will do', the slogans of Rothman's rivals. Furthermore, he wanted to sell it for around 40 cents a packet, which not only sliced the profit margin but could rebound on the company because smokers might consider it a cheap, and therefore possibly inferior, product, so conditioned had they been to so-called quality. The task of preparing a campaign was given to the Sydney advertising company Herz-Walpole.

The first thing Jim Walpole, who took over the campaign, looked for was an acceptable Australian to sell the product, which was to be called Winfield. His eye fell on Hogan. After long negotiations and not a little haggling, Hogan and Cornell agreed. There were several reasons why Hogan appealed, not the least his commercial virginity – that is, he had never appeared in a television commercial before, or in any other advertisement for that matter. It was a risk Walpole thought worth taking. Next he had to sell Hogan to Rothman's. This was done in the way Hogan usually did things – by

being Hoges. A black and white film was shot in which Hogan, work boots up on the director's desk, sniffing, scratching his ear, drinking from a beer can, chatted amiably to Watson, calling him Reg and telling him that he, Hogan, was in control of the situation and knew the right formula. Rothman's had suggested that the selling slogan should be: 'Anywhere, anytime, anyhow have a Winfield.' Hogan replied that it should be shaved to the more easy-going 'Anyhow . . . have a Winfield.'

After seeing the film clip of Hogan, Watson turned to Walpole, who was understandably nervous because his idea was breaking new grounds in advertising. 'Who's that fellow?' Watson asked.

'He's a rigger on the Harbour Bridge,' said Walpole, fingers crossed.

'He's a very good salesman,' Watson said. 'Entirely credible and brand spanking new.'

Walpole confessed later: 'We sort of put our reputation on the line doing it this way – we could have been thrown out on our ear after they had seen the film. As it was they gave it a terrific reception.'

Hogan was contracted for a signing fee of about $10,000, going to $30,000 for the second contract. Considering he was getting little more than $100 a week, it was big money. The commercials were written to show Hogan not in shorts and boots cracking dunny jokes, but performing a gentle satire on the Australian character.

In his first commercial he was shown in a dinner suit conducting the 50-piece Sydney Symphony Orchestra, an ordinary man's sophisticate, the bloke from down the road totally in control even when he entered the world of classical music, in this case Tchaikovsky's. He also appeared as a concert pianist. For this one, Hogan himself suggested changes to the script because, as he pointed out, he knew Australians as good, if not better, than most. One of his suggestions had him turning to the conductor and saying, 'Let 'er rip, Boris,' an expression that went into the idiom. The original line by the advertising agency was, 'Let 'em have it, Boris.' Hogan's subtle change had much greater impact.

Hogan likes to tell the story of filming with the orchestra.

You've got to remember I can't play much more than a banjo. Some of the camera shots were taken from directly above the piano and you can see the dampers movin' as it's played. So in case there's any real musical buffs watching, they've got to have a proper pianist playing so the correct dampers will be movin'. They get this orchestra pianist and he sat on the floor beneath the piano with his hands on the keys and a black bag over his head so the camera wouldn't spot him. I was sittin' at the stool with me legs on top of his head.

It's a terrible complicated shot and the cameraman said to me: 'Hell, Hogan, if you hadn't wasted the last ten years crawling around the Harbour Bridge and learned to play the piano instead, we wouldn't have had to go to this trouble.'

And I said, 'If I'd spent the last ten years learning' to play the piano I'd be sittin' on the floor with some other prawn's foot on me head.'

The commercial was astonishingly successful – the advertising industry concedes that it was the most successful campaign ever in Australia – the sales of Winfield cigarettes rocketed from nowhere to a good share of the market. The only criticism of the advertisement came from an unexpected quarter. 'It was me mother-in-law. After she saw the commercials, she said, "You dress nice, but I wish you'd talk properly." Talk properly! Gawd, they only sell 300,000 cigarettes a month.'

Hogan continued with a series of commercials that put him in different situations – parachuting from a plane, skippering a luxury yacht, flying through the air as a circus trapeze artist. All the commercials worked but the best was the original showing him conducting the orchestra.

Some commercials required stunts, and Hogan liked to do them himself if possible. In one filmed near Cairns, North Queensland, he risked his life by diving 30 feet down the face of a waterfall and then being swept along for 100 feet by 30 mph rapids, to be caught by a safety net on the brink of another waterfall.

He admitted that when he saw the location he took a step backwards. It was planned that a stuntman should do the dive, but his efforts didn't look right. The stuntman was fine in the water but wasn't able to dive with the style of a hero. Enter Hogan, the star of afternoon sessions at the Granville Olympic Swimming Pool, the daredevil who had risked life and limb countless times on the high board.

'I reckon I can do it,' he said.

'I dunno. Could be a bit risky.'

'She'll be right. The divin' bit's a piece of cake.'

Halfway down the thought struck Hogan, 'You're mad. You're not as young as you used to be.' He hit the water and it was freezing. An icy jolt went through him. But he did not have time to worry about the temperature because the current caught him and whisked him along like a scrap of paper in a gale. Then he hit the net and, looking anxiously at the water roaring down a rock-strewn fall a few yards further on, grasped it tightly until he was hauled out.

'Very good, Paul. Now we'll do it again.'

'Again?'

And again and again. 'I had to do it about five times before we got it exactly right. I reckon I earned my dough.'

Even his brother Pat became involved in the Winfield commercials. Returning to Canada,

With brother Pat (left): 'not only suave and sophisticated like meself' but on hand to help Hoges launch a new cigarette.

he was signed to do a series of advertisements which had Hogan saying: 'Meet me brother Pat. He's not only suave and sophisticated like meself, but after travellin' the world for the last ten years he's developed a taste for extra mild smokin', so I brought 'im out here to give me a hand to launch these new fags.'

The only problem was that Pat could not cope with being a relative of Hoges – in other words, expected to perform whenever he appeared in public. After a while he left Australia. 'He spends most of his time wanderin' around the world,' explained Hogan, 'because when he's in a pub here someone recognizes him and expects him to do a Hogan routine. He can't handle that.'

True to its word, the Labour Government banned the advertising of tobacco on television and radio but the Winfield commercials appeared in cinemas and Hogan's face was on street posters. Winfield's share of the adult market reached 28 per cent, more than double that of its Benson & Hedges rival. But what alarmed people in certain quarters was that half of the schoolchildren who smoked preferred Winfield. In 1980 the chairman of the Advertising Standards Council, Sir Richard Kirby, banned Hogan from promoting Winfield. He said Hogan was simply too popular with children, but emphasized that this had 'grown with his general popularity without sinister undertones of endeavouring to initiate or encourage smoking by the young. There has been nothing put before me which in any way adversely reflects upon Mr Hogan.'

As the Winfield billboards began coming down across Australia, Hogan indignantly retorted:

The ruling amounts to being sent off the field for kickin' too many goals. They have ruled that you can promote a product but you can't do it too well. I don't believe I ever encouraged a kid to take up smoking. I don't believe I was ever lookin' down like some Svengali from a poster saying, 'Go and buy a packet of cigarettes.' The Winfield ads were always carefully designed to appeal to smokers, not to non-smokers. The message was, 'If you smoke, this is the brand you should be smoking,' not 'Go out and take it up because it's good for you.'

Winfield gave Hogan's career an enormous boost. Until the cigarette commercials appeared on television he was known only in Sydney and Melbourne, the two cities where *A Current Affair* was shown, and then only to those who chose to watch the show. The commercials gave him national exposure. Oddly, more than a decade later commercials, this time for beer and tourism, were to give him international exposure, making him perhaps the only international star to become known around the world through plugging products on television. His case would have fascinated Marshall McLuhan.

After the first of the Winfield commercials came the first of his own television shows. Hogan and Cornell decided they could make people laugh on a bigger scale than was possible in two or three minutes on a current affairs programme. They started developing an hour-long show. It wasn't easy. For one thing, neither had had experience in television variety production; they were going into an unknown area which had more traps than a rabbit-infested property. Unlike in Britain or America, where they could have called upon people experienced in comedy and variety, they had to start essentially from scratch . . . from nowhere. About the only man who could handle comedy was Jimmy Fishburn, for several years a director of television variety and producer of the *Mavis Bramston Show*, a satirical programme popular a decade previously. 'We had to make it up as we went and take the risk of hiring people who hadn't done that sort of work before. It was a crash learning process,' said Hogan.

Fishburn suggested they go on the road to gain experience and from out of that, from performances at clubs and pubs and theatres, came a small ensemble company which formed the basis of the first Hogan shows.

'What I liked about him was that he had a new approach,' said Fishburn. 'The man's a professional from top to bottom; you felt that the first moment you talked to him. His attitude to audiences was one of the things I

With manager John Cornell (right). Cornell has total faith in Hogan's ability. Though he too lacks a showbiz background, he has always seen the potential for developing Hogan's talent.

Filming *Hogan Abroad* in Singapore.

liked best. He didn't treat them as fools. He didn't under-estimate them and say, "I'll get away with this one." '

His first show, for TCN9, relied heavily on the Hoges character. There were many ocker jokes and sketches in which ockers triumphed over authority, a favourite theme in Australian comedy. Because of the Winfield commercials, a fair-sized audience tuned in, but the show hardly set the world on fire. Hogan and Cornell decided to venture abroad. The ocker in exotic and faraway places was guaranteed to produce laughs. They went to Singapore to tape one called *Hogan Abroad (or How to Travel Overseas without Making a Mug of Yourself)*. It was roughly made and when aired did not receive favourable attention. They went further abroad, this time to London. An ocker among the Poms had more possibilities and Hogan seized them eagerly. He liked London,

although he thought the Poms didn't have much imagination because 'they've pinched most of their street names off the Monopoly board.' He also observed that 'British sheilas are bigger than Australian sheilas. It's because they have to work harder to breathe through all the smog, y'know.'

Even though it was one of the costliest shows ever made for Australian television, it was, in fact, shot on a shoestring when compared with the budgets of shows made in other countries.

We wanted to film a sequence outside Buckingham Palace but the coppers refused permission. So we sneaked there at seven o'clock in the morning. We were wearin' our ocker gear with our coats over the top of it. There's a copper walkin' up and down his beat. We both stand in front of the palace gates and the cameraman stands opposite with a zoom lens and two blokes stand in front of him reading newspapers so the camera can't be spotted. When the copper reaches the end of his beat, we drop the overcoats and stand in the ocker gear, chattin' away to the viewers. As the copper turns around, we slip the coats on again and walk along clicking away with our little Brownies.

Receiving permission to film at Madame Tussaud's, home of the world's finest collection of dummies, they were dismayed to find they could not do a particular segment they had sketched out – one in which Hogan chatted up the waxwork figures of the royal family. 'So we drew straws to get one of our blokes to chat up the bird who was the caretaker. He really had to turn on the charm and work her into a corner so we could sneak up among the waxworks and talk to 'em. It worked. We got what we wanted and no one was any wiser.'

The plot for his London special, if indeed it had a plot, was that, having solved all the problems of Australia, Hogan was asked by the British Prime Minister, Ted Heath, to come and sort out Britain. Naturally the first person he consulted was the great television bigot, Alf Garnett, played by Warren Mitchell. The sequence involving Alf was filmed in

If there were such a thing as an English ocker, Alf Garnett, portrayed by Warren Mitchell, would surely qualify as one (1976).

the Dover Castle, a pub in the West End, on a Sunday morning, when it was crowded with regulars, none of whom knew Hogan from a pint of bitter. But they soon caught on to the Hogan humour and Cornell, as usual keeping a cagey eye on things, noted that Hogan's jokes and style travelled well. It was something to file for later reference. Alf told Hoges that he didn't think much of his convict stock, 'not that you can help it if your father was a bit light-fingered,' he added.

'It's a real pleasure to meet an intelligent man like yourself,' said Hoges, 'particularly one who has such an interest in a country that isn't even his own.'

'Not my own? What do you mean? I'm true-blue British,' said Alf indignantly.

'What, with that nose you must be kidding!'

Apart from being manager and co-writer, Cornell had by now gone in front of the cameras as a character called Strop, a dill who admired Hoges as the source of all wisdom. Cornell had no ambitions to be a comic but was forced into the business because of tight budgets. 'He used to do a party trick, an impression of Marlon Brando in *The God-father*,' said Hogan:

It was a very bad imitation. Mike Willesee wanted a piece about the Mafia, who were supposed to be worming their way into the markets. Hoges decided he needed a stooge to infiltrate the markets himself. Bein' a low-budget show, we couldn't afford actors, so I got John to dress up. We gave him a bottle of plonk and a salami and he stuffed toilet paper in his cheeks like Brando and pushed out his jaw like Brando and the result was – Strop! He was a useful sort of character and he's gradually developed since then as we've given him a bit of personality, but not too much – seein' how dopey he is.

After a dispute with TCN9, Hogan switched to another Sydney station, ATN7. The ratings grew and, ironically, in 1974 he soundly trounced Michael Willesee, the man who gave him his start in television. Their programmes ran against each other on one night, with Hogan attracting 37 per cent of viewers and Willesee 17 per cent. A Frank Sinatra special

Hogan finds writing comedy scripts hard work, but still writes much of his own material.

on the third commercial channel drew, incidentally, a mere 16 per cent.

The public obviously liked him but the critics still thought he wasn't worth two shakes of a dead lamb's tail. According to Charles Wright, in *The Australian*:

Anybody who has watched the Paul Hogan show over the past few months will of course have completely overlooked the evidence it so eloquently presents of the fact that Paul Hogan has not ventured out into the real world for years and years and years . . .

Sandra Hall in *The Bulletin* thought Hogan's material was 'getting more threadbare by the month and it's looking even worse than it ought to be because it's being played so badly . . .'

With money at last coming in, Hogan and Cornell ventured into other enterprises. One was a restaurant and discotheque called Aphrodisia Rhythm Restaurant. Hogan pointed out that Hoges wouldn't be a patron. 'He goes to places where the food is crook and the staff acts like they're doing you a favour. Not like this place.' Although set up well enough to attract the gold-chain brigade, it didn't find favour and Hogan and Cornell moved on to other ventures. One was a classical record. Actually it was a recording of the Paris Orchestra playing Prokofiev's *Peter and the Wolf*, with Hogan narrating the story in his own colourful language. For instance, instead of saying the wolf ate the duck he said 'the duck went down like the first cold turkey at a butcher's picnic.'

He was the darling of the tabloid press which, unlike its serious counterparts, had no hang-ups about the popularity of ockerism, and used him whenever possible. One Sydney Sunday newspaper got him to write a television column criticizing his own show, an opportunity that perhaps even Olivier or Gielgud would have enjoyed. The *Sunday Telegraph* took him to the NSW Art Gallery to view the Jackson Pollock masterpiece 'Blue Poles', a controversial work made more so by the fact that Gough Whitlam's Federal Government had purchased it for $1.3 million, an unheard-of amount in those days. The tabloid press had a field day when it discovered that

Pollock, the leading American painter of abstract expressionism, was an alcoholic who used a technique in which he dribbled paint over the canvas. 'Drunk Did It!' screamed a Sydney *Daily Mirror* poster. It was a fine time for ockers and Hogan joined in.

It's bloody incredible. Gough must have been full, was he? Chalky Hill, who works on the bridge, would have knocked up something like that for about $25. They oughta sell it now before the world wakes up. Only a poser and a goose could go for this. If Gough thinks it's fantastic, Gough's a goose. Old Jack Pollock finished up with 'Blue Poles' because there was more blue paint on his brush than any other colour. It looks like the mess I've seen in the paintshop down at the bridge. I'm thinkin' of slipping back to the bridge, chipping it off the wall and stickin' it up here.

The artistic community groaned. Most of the public agreed with Hogan, even if it was Hoges talking, sending up those he believed were posers. 'Blue Poles' is now worth $7 million and is one of the main attractions at the National Gallery, Canberra. Hogan's contributions to the print media were carefully planned to keep the public amused between television appearances. When he was in England the Sydney *Sun* printed some of his observations on life:

FOOD: one of the favourite things I like to put in me mouth. Very fond of Chinese, especially the odd Chiko Roll and curried prawns. A tip: always use a knife and fork. Use chopsticks only if you're on a diet – chopsticks are the reason the Chinese are so skinny. The food keeps dropping off 'em. You'd think the poor devils would have woken up to that by now. Italian food's not bad either, especially the spaghetti bolognaise that Heinz puts out. The tins are real easy to open. Greek food is what I like best after the real Australian nosh like steak and eggs. Chris the Greek at his café down the corner serves the best hamburgers outside of Athens.

WOMEN: the second most important item in a bedroom. A great invention and I'd like to congratulate whoever was responsible for the design . . .

POMS: possibly me favourite foreigners 'cos they do try to speak English pretty good. You gotta give 'em a go seein' as a lot of their descendants come from here. And remember that any race that invented sandwiches can't be mugs.

SPORT: like all games. Me favourite is Rugby League, but I'm no slouch at cricket either, gained from years of experience coaching on the Hill [cheapest public section of Sydney Cricket Ground]. I reckon cricket needs brightening up a bit. My solution is to let the players drink at the beginning of the game, not after. It always works at our picnic matches.

CLOTHES: it's easy to look well dressed as long as you remember me golden rules. Never wear socks with thongs [type of cheap sandal]. Never put polish on your shoes – it can make the rest of your clothes look grotty. If you're goin' to a posh do always wear your footy jumper under your shirt.

MYSELF: modest, philanthropic, a sage with a heart of gold, all me own teeth. Always ready to share me wisdom and skill with others not so fortunate.

In his early television days Hogan sometimes looked at his successes, the Jaguar car, the swimming pool, the money in the bank, and could not believe it was happening to him, a former rigger, a knockabout whose wallet had contained little more than moths for most of his early working life. Nor could he believe that his show was now employing the same big names in Australian television that he had watched, and admired, in his Chullora home. There had been such a dramatic turnabout in his life that now and again he thought he might wake up and find himself back on the bridge.

'He was astonished that he was successful,' said Jimmy Fishburn.

He said he used to pinch himself [to make sure] that it wasn't a dream. And in a way he was a little awe-struck by some of the stars we put him with. While he was still on the bridge he used to watch them and all of a sudden they were performing in his show. He was never shy but at the same time you could see there was a slight embarrassment, hoping that everything was all right. After a while he realized they respected him as much as he respected them. Another thing I liked about him was in the six years I was with him he never lost his temper. Not ever, ever, ever. If you had a different point of view, whether he agreed with you or not, he would let you have your say. If you were adamant on one thing and he was just as adamant, he would look for a compromise. He'd say, let's do it both ways and see which one works.

The A-team of *The Paul Hogan Show*: Hogan with John Cornell in his 'Strop' outfit and Mrs Cornell, Delvene Delaney.

Hogan and Cornell wrote most of the early material, at times using other writers like Ken Shadie. It may have looked easy on the screen but it wasn't so when confronted by a blank piece of paper. Hogan had never studied the art of scriptwriting, any sort of writing, but taught himself as he went along. 'I sit down with a pad and a blunt pencil and let it all come out,' he said. 'I overwrite to hell and John comes along later and edits it. That seems to work out pretty well. Sometimes it comes easy, sometimes I have to sweat for days. I wrote three sketches for the first show in one afternoon. The other stuff I write comes nowhere as easily.'

Scrutinizing the work of established comedians, he searched for their strengths and weaknesses, concluding that brevity is the soul of wit.

I've been looking at a lot and one thing I've learned is that they shouldn't go on too long. Even Marty Feldman [now dead], who's supposed to be the best, lets some run on too long. I think the trouble comes when you make an hour show and you've got only half an hour of material. That's the kiss of death . . . You're not there to educate people or try to make 'em think. You've basically got to make 'em laugh. It doesn't matter how you do it. People have this funny attitude where they seem to think that to do sophisticated humour you have to wear a dinner suit and bow-tie and tell dirty jokes.

Hogan was not an admirer of comics such as Bob Hope who stood in the spotlight rattling off jokes written by others. But he liked the American comedian Don Rickles – and for a very novel reason.

You watch him for half an hour and you can't steal any of his act because there aren't any gags. There's nothin' you can go and tell the blokes at the pub afterwards. What he says isn't really jokes. He deals mainly in personal insults, but it's the way he does them. He gives people heaps. Anyone else saying such things would get a smack in the mouth, but he makes them funny. The only thing I don't like about Rickles' act is the way he squares off at the end by saying' we're all brothers under the skin and I really love you all. He should leave the bucket dropped on everyone!

Because in show business originality is merely something to be copied, others soon latched on to Hogan's ocker image. There were ockers everywhere. You couldn't step out your front door without falling over ockers. They were on television selling goods from paint to groceries, from holidays to motor cars. They were in clubs yabbering about dunnies and chundering. There were singing ockers and dancing ockers. Australian show business had never seen so many ockers. It was one of the few things that riled Hogan.

A lot of these galahs are comin' on now and acting like ockers. It's their gimmick. My gimmick was that I *was* an ocker. I didn't come on and try to pretend I was an ocker to be funny. I don't like seein' blokes talking about having the backside out of their pants if they've never really had it out. I'm not there to try and convince them I'm a good fellow. I'm not one of those pathetic creatures that's always appealing, 'Please like me,' because I don't give a stuff if they like me or not – as long as they laugh.

He had no objection to one group that tried to cash in on his success. Three Harbour Bridge painters, Derek Quinn, Vili Drazenovic and Chris Chambers, calling themselves the Bridge Painters Harmony Trio, released a record, 'Our Paul Hogan Doesn't Roll His Own'.

Rip all your sleeves off, peroxide your hair,
And you're nearly there.
Paul, Paul, you're our mate . . .
Paul, Paul, we think you're great . . .

It didn't exactly set the record industry on fire.

The only hiccup in those early years was when he collapsed with acute appendicitis on an aircraft flying to Melbourne. He was ordered to rest for three weeks.

By now Hogan had moved with his family from Chullora to a house in the much more expensive and leafier North Shore, then moved again when the house became well known. After late-night parties revellers would roar past the house in their cars shouting, 'Good on yer, Hoges,' which did nothing for the Hogan family's sleep. 'People started comin' around and having picnics on me front yard,' he complained. 'They would come and gape at us for hours. Sometimes they'd send the kids in for an autograph. One night about

On location for an episode of *The Paul Hogan Show*.

eight o'clock a woman arrived at the front door wanting Kamahl's [a singer's] address. I told her I wouldn't know Kamahl from a bar of soap. "Yer must," she said. "Youse all knock around together." '

They moved again, this time to a house hidden from the road by tall trees and shrubs, but a bushfire destroyed the foliage and the tourists began stopping outside the house.

'I've given up,' he said resignedly to Jerry Fetherston of *TV Week*.

Don't get me wrong, it's not that I don't like recognition and the people are friendly, never nasty. But there are times when you'd just like to be yourself – a gawker and not a gawkee, if you know what I mean . . . People say to me I must be out of touch because I'm livin' in a big house in a posh suburb. But I'm not out of touch, it's bred into you. There's an old saying: 'You can take the kid out of the gutter but you can't take the gutter out of the kid.'

The Hogans' privacy wasn't helped when one of their sons began bringing children to the house, like the bus tours of the homes of Hollywood celebrities, for 10 cents a time,

Hogan with wife Noelene and baby Scott in June, 1973. The proud dad likened his new son to a baby prawn.

which included an autographed photograph of Hogan. For 50 cents those interested could obtain the unlisted telephone number of their television hero. Hogan had to put a stop to it. 'It gets a bit embarrassin' coming home to a house full of kids who just stand there gawkin' at you.'

In June, 1973 the Hogans had another child, a boy, Scott David, to join Brett (thirteen), Clay (twelve), Todd (eleven) and Laureen (four). 'He looks like a baby prawn,' Hogan joked to the media representatives gathered for the first photographs of the boy. 'Strewth, he's ugly. He's got more wrinkles than his old man. But we Hogans always start that way. We're late developers when it comes to good looks.' The photographic session was rare because Hogan tried hard to keep his family from

publicity. He argued he was the one in the public eye, not his wife and kids, and refused many requests to do the family-album type of picture spread so beloved of women's magazines.

Hogan was happy with his new life, with the money that came in, the opportunity to give his children a much better life than would have been possible had he stayed on the bridge. But sometimes Noelene had her doubts. 'I didn't like the celebrity bit at all,' she said in 1975.

I find it very hard to talk to people. It frightened me at first, all the publicity and pictures in the paper and people mobbing Paul in shops. I was a bit frightened he might change. But he hasn't. He's still the same – he's just a big kid at heart. The hardest thing to take was not having Paul home in the evenings. He used to come home at five o'clock every day from the bridge. That all changed when we went on TV and he had to come home at all sorts of odd hours. I found it very hard to adjust to him not being there for the first few months. Now it's good because I have him home in the mornings.

A decade later the newspaper columnist and critic Phillip Adams suggested that the Hogans were uncomfortable in their new life. Adams recalled a moment when the Hogans were wandering around the building site of a mansion they were constructing on the outskirts of Sydney.

'Everything's perfect,' Hogan said to his wife.

'Except for us,' said Noelene. 'We don't fit.'

One suspects there may have been a joke in there somewhere that Adams missed. Hogan made no bones about preferring a mansion to a fibro cottage.

Nor, as the money came in, did he turn his back on his old mates from the Harbour Bridge and Chullora days. One day an old friend looked up Hogan and said: 'Sorry to bother you, Paul, but I badly need a loan.'

'How much?' asked Hogan.

'Six hundred dollars.'

'All right,' said Hogan. 'I'll have to give you a cheque. I haven't got that much on me in cash.'

He wrote the cheque. The next day his mate returned and handed him back the cheque. 'I didn't need the money,' he said. 'I was just testing you to see if you'd changed.'

*'I've got bludging down to a fine art
. . . I enjoy being lazy and I'm really
good at it.'*
Paul Hogan

Paul Hogan knew that one day he would have to stab a dear friend in the back. He put off the decision but in 1975 he realized he could no longer hold back and he acted. He gave Hoges the shove. As Hogan put it: 'The singlet and boots thing has done its bit.'

To be truthful, the ocker character was not totally put out to pasture but was used sparingly. He'd had a good run, had provided well for the Hogan family, but it had become harder and harder to extend the joke. Furthermore, Hogan, encouraged by Cornell, who would tell anyone who cared to listen that Hogan was one of the greatest talents loose on this planet, wanted to prove he was more than a one-dimensional comedian, a performer with one joke that was repeated over and over again like a politician's promise. 'I've changed a lot over the years – matured, I suppose – and got myself a lot more of an idea of what this business is about and what I should be doing,' he said at the time. He pointed to Benny Hill and Dick Emery as comedians who tended to be repetitive, though he admired the way they worked.

Hogan began introducing characters into his show, all of whom he played himself. One of

Hoges and 'Strop' (John Cornell), on-screen double-act and off-screen business partnership. Their professional relationship was founded on a handshake.

the most popular was Luigi the Unbelievable, a magician whose tricks were as transparent as glass. Another was Nigel Lovelace, an 11-year-old bikie on a skateboard. 'Think of everything that's crass and objectionable, mean and a little nasty, dress him like a bikie, stick him on a board and you've got Nigel.'

One character who caused a stir was Smithy, portrayed as a war veteran who had been no closer to the heat of battle than in his armchair watching a John Wayne movie on television.

Luigi the Unbelievable – one of life's posers, whose antics can always be relied upon not to impress.

He . . . tells lies about the war he has never been in and brags about his battle conquests. He has never left Australia's shores, but Smithy always fought courageously under the country's flag. He lies about everything and drinks free on his war stories. He always tells the best war stories, because he was a Spitfire pilot or a submarine commander. He says he's a lot of other things, too. He always asks around the bar if anyone knows anythin' about submarines or Spitfires. When people give him a negative answer Smithy says 'Good, I meself fought under Australia's flag,' and starts to lie and brag.

Some of the more red-necked members of the RSL didn't think Smithy was funny at all. Nor was a politician, Bruce Webster, amused when Hogan ran a sketch called 'Bloodbath Telemovie of the Week', featuring the Vampire Cubs, which was meant to be little more than a spoof on horror movies. The cub scouts helped little old ladies across the street, as is their duty, then attacked them for their blood. Webster said it denigrated the cub scout movement and that Hogan's send-up was 'a cowardly act'. A popular character was Detective Donger. Corrupt and brutal, Donger's appeal said much about the Australian attitude to law enforcement in general and the police force in particular. The public looked at Donger, who owing to an accident had had his beer gut replaced with a bionic stomach, noted his corrupt, bullying ways, and thought, 'Yeah, that's about right.'

Less successful was the bush philosopher, whom Hogan portrayed sitting by a campfire delivering a monologue on life. 'He only did two or three of those sketches. The public wasn't ready for them,' said Jimmy Fishburn. 'As much as Paul liked it, he thought his audiences didn't and he put it on the back-burner. I believe the character was the one who became "Crocodile" Dundee.'

Part of the show was shot outdoors, occasionally providing some interesting moments. Hospital administrators complained when they saw a man in scuba-diving gear carrying a speargun and menacing a scantily-clad nurse. Another of his characters, Perce the Wino, a derelict drunk with a sense of humour, was forever being harassed by other derelicts when segments were filmed on location. Other derelicts demanded a swig or two from his bottle of booze or offered to share their bottle, sometimes containing methylated spirits laced with orange drink, and householders rang to ask the police to remove the 'drunk' from their back lane. During a break in filming in Fitzroy Gardens, Melbourne, Hogan took the opportunity to visit the men's lavatory. As he came out, he was surrounded by a group of young schoolchildren on an excursion. A horrified teacher didn't recognize Hogan in his wino gear and frantically tried to keep the children away.

'It's all right,' the children. said to the teacher. 'It's Hoges.'

'No, it's not,' the teacher yelled. 'Get away from him. Go on!'

Perce was Hogan's favourite character of that period.

As Perce I can roll in the gutter, get run over and sit on the ground and I can't ruin the wardrobe. Not only that, people react to Perce, particularly when we film in the street. As Perce in London [later] I would wander all over the place tippin' me hat, smilin' – then stand back and watch people be almost sick. They'd walk away and brush off their clothes where I'd touched them.

A young actress called Delvene Delaney became a regular on the show, her rôles ranging from filling out a bikini for an ogling scene to that of a 70-year-old woman. She had been working in London in the Playboy Club and returned home as 'one of those affected young ladies with a half-English accent. So when I saw Paul on television I just about died.' She recalled one night when they had been out filming and arrived at their hotel still in make-up:

The sketch was the one about cub scouts being vampires. I'd been required to dress up as a 70-year-old woman. When we reached the hotel, Paul dragged me by the arm and pushed me through the door shouting, 'Get in there, you old bag.' As I lay there grovelling for my cane the doorman came sprinting up, looking as white as a sheet. I got to my feet and we all started laughing.

(text continues on page 120)

Hoges' Gallery

Appealing to our more primitive instincts?

Never mind the Sex Pistols . . .

'David Carradine' of *Kung Fu* fame.

In Elizabethan guise for a Merrie England sketch.

That *can't* have been the amber nectar, surely?

'Rudolf Nureyev' – look, the feller with no strides on!

Foreseeing an exciting future? Hogan as super-sage Nostradamus.

'Mr Spock' contemplates another stellar journey.

The noblest Roman?

As a change from bowling the ladies over, Hogan became a lady bowler for one of his TV sketches.

'Conan the Barbarian'.

'Indiana Jones' – eat your heart out,
Harrison . . .

Was *Hawaii Five-O* really like this?

Ever-vigilant tough-guy 'Charles Bronson'.

'The Phantom', with Delvene Delaney occupying the leopard skin.

**Hogan, with the Big Red Book and entertainer
Don Lane.**

He cannot be serious! Hogan takes on super-brat McEnroe.

'Rod Stewart' – well, *do* you think he's sexy?

Delaney and Cornell married on New Year's Eve, 1977, in a ceremony that (considering those involved) had to be, and was, different from the usual stroll down the aisle. It took place at midnight, when the rest of the country was singing 'Auld Lang Syne', on a farm on the north coast of New South Wales, the marriage celebrant having been directed to turn off the highway at the second kangaroo sign in order to reach the farm. The vows were made under a 100-year-old pear tree, the bride was barefoot, the farm's electrical generator provided the background 'music' and, apart from close relatives, the wedding was observed by a dog and a big white horse called Moriarty.

Hogan left ATN7 and returned to TCN9, mainly because the latter station, through its Melbourne and Sydney Nine Network, offered bigger budgets, better facilities and Peter Faiman, the country's best variety director, who went on to direct 'Crocodile' Dundee. Hogan's contract with Kerry Packer, the Nine Network chief, ignored Sam Goldwyn's dictum that 'A verbal contract isn't worth the paper it's written on': it was merely a handshake, with nothing on paper. The contract was also unique in that Hogan could determine how many shows he could produce each year. At one stage he was making seven; soon it was down to three. He admitted that he would rather be stretched out beside the swimming pool or kicking a football with the kids than sweating it out writing and performing. 'Basically I'm a bludger,' he told journalist Kevin Sadlier.

I've got bludging down to a fine art. You're a long time dead so enjoy life when you can. I enjoy being lazy and I'm really good at it. I make excuses to myself about why I don't do this and why I don't do that, but what it all boils down to is I'm bone lazy. There's a chance I won't do anythin' at all next year . . . I like to get up when I wake up, eat me breakfast, go for a swim, read the papers – that's what I like. I really do believe in smellin' the roses.

His old mate, Athol Gilmore, agreed. 'He's fundamentally lazy. I saw him on one of those talk shows and they said, "What are you doing?" and he said, "Bludgin' ". The whole audience laughed. But he wasn't joking. He meant it.'

Hogan soon proved he had made the right move when he switched television stations by getting record ratings figures. Never satisfied with their product, Hogan and Cornell kept changing the characters and Hogan moved further into the art of impersonation, taking off show-business personalities and movie stars. To pick up their idiosyncrasies, Hogan spent hours studying film clips, then several more hours in the make-up department. He must have been doing something right because he won several Logie Awards, a sort of Australian Emmy, given by *TV Week*. At that stage Hogan had no great ambition to become an international star. Of course he sometimes talked about it with Cornell, and together they dreamed of new ventures, but the ideas developed no further. When he did move beyond Australian shores, the decision was forced on him. The reason was the old Australian problem of a limited population. When Hogan realized he had virtually run out of Australian show-business personalities to impersonate, he widened his range to include Elvis Presley, John McEnroe, Charles Bronson, Mr Spock of *Star Trek*, Rod Stewart and 'Conan the Barbarian'. While the essential Australian flavour remained, it was not long before the show's wider appeal was being reflected in comments and letters from overseas visitors to Australia who believed his work would travel.

Talking to Neil Lawrence and Steve Bunk for *The Stump-Jumpers* (1985), Hogan made the international move sound easy. It wasn't. No entertainer has found gaining a toehold in international show business any easy proposition. He said that through 1979 and 1980 he broadened the show so that 20 per cent of the material was for purely Australian consumption, the rest had an international theme able to be understood anywhere. By the end of 1980 he had enough material to edit into 26 half-hour shows he believed could work around the world. An English international distributor, Richard Price, sold them to Britain and the United States, eventually dubbing them into six or seven different languages for release in 30 countries. Many an Australian traveller, switching on the television in a hotel room in Spain or Thailand and watching with astonishment his favourite ocker holding forth

Big Rolf (Harris) and Little Rolf.

in another tongue would have given his last dollar to be able to understand the translation of 'Don't come the raw prawn' or possibly 'He shot through like a Bondi tram.' Hogan said he wasn't surprised by the overseas success of his show. 'You see, most of those shows were cut to visual unity,' he said in *The Stump-Jumpers*.

For instance, a wino wandering down the street doesn't even talk. He doesn't have to be in Australia to do the things he does. It's a sight gag, just like Charlie Chaplin did. They laugh at that in Spain, Japan or wherever. They don't put Hogan on in other countries because he used to work on the Harbour Bridge and is therefore a bit of a legend; they put him on because he's funny.. And it's got nothin' to do with whether they like Aussies or not. Those punters couldn't care less where it came from, as long as it's funny.

For a few dollars more, it's 'Clint' . . .

The ever-enthusiastic Cornell predicted a big future for Hogan on American television. But then Hogan only had to burp for Cornell to declare it a major breakthrough in comic behaviour. 'Everyone who has seen the show in America is tremendously excited,' he said. 'They are all predicting it will be a big, big hit . . . What struck me about Hogan as I looked through all those old shows was the tremendous improvement he has shown over the years. They confirmed what I had always thought – that Hogan is world-class.' However, the early shows had a limited run in Los Angeles and New York, attracting a cult following but not a great response from the general public. That was to come.

With glamorous Delvene Delaney, who once worked in the London Playboy Club.

Duet by smoothie Hoges and a *Hogan*-show regular.

In Britain, the début of *The Paul Hogan Show* was more successful. A series of them was used to help launch Channel 4 in November, 1982. The critics were poised, Hogan appeared and they struck.

The *Times*' television critic commented: 'The Paul Hogan Show* is reputed to be the channel's "hot property", although it really might have been picked up in a lost and found department. All we saw was an Australian comedian wearing a torn shirt with arms like tree trunks and a manner wooden enough to reinforce them. He sounded very much like a butch Benny Hill, all beer and belching with an audience laughing hysterically at the slightest sexual innuendo.' Its sister publication, *The Sunday Times*, was equally bitchy: 'The sight gags – much speeded-up film and scatology – are embarrassingly limp and much of the material too parochial or hopelessly dated. Some of the shows in the series are three years old. The running gag is a grotesquely over-weight and over-exposed female.' The *Financial Times* thought Hogan had 'the ability of a Jasper Carrott or a Dave Allen to go before an audience and re-live the embarrassing moment [trying to chat up a dental nurse while your lip is anaesthetized] with devastating accuracy.' *The Guardian* observed: 'In-born bad taste attracted me strongly to Paul Hogan . . . he is known as Hoges to his friends, among whom he numbers – or did – one Dingbat Hilton, who jumped off the Parramatta railway bridge with 53 pigeons sticky-taped to his arms to prove that man could fly.' The *Daily Mail* complained: 'Paul Hogan has been launched as a potential crowd-pleaser, although I confess I didn't once twitch a smile muscle.'

But Rupert Murdoch's *Sun*, Britain's biggest-selling daily, was enthusiastic. This had nothing to do with Murdoch and Hogan being Australians; rather, it was *The Sun*'s well-honed instinct for material with mass appeal. *The Sun* said: 'The Paul Hogan Show was a beaut, as they say Down Under. Despite his fondness for a four-letter word rarely heard on TV over here (it's "wank", if you must know), and a tendency to mention obscure Aussie politicians, Hogan is a real hero of comedy. His divorce sketch, with the bride and groom throwing unwanted presents back at their guests, was a stroke of genius.'

Noting the scathing reviews and, incidentally, ignoring those that were complimentary, Hogan sighed. They were almost a repeat of his early television days in Australia, but what saved him from wondering if it was all worth it was an unshaken belief in his own ability, and that of the British to laugh. He had often said the English knew comedy better than anyone, perhaps even invented it, their one fault being a tendency to take it too seriously. For instance they analysed Hogan's humour, which he had never done himself, believing that the more it was analysed the less funny it became, and he was surprised when they found things in his work he never knew were there. His faith in himself was vindicated when the ratings came out; they showed good, if not strong, public support for his show.

With the international market now of major importance, and encouraged by such experienced performers as David Frost and Michael

Hogan with Dennis Lillee (right) and Rod Marsh, for *Paul Hogan's England*, an Australian TV special.

Parkinson, he produced two shows in England, poking fun at British history by giving an ocker slant to such events as King Alfred and the burnt cakes ('I told 'em to give them 10 minutes more') and King Canute ('I said you hold the tide and I'll get the worms'). There was Perce the Wino on the skids in St James's Park and World Cup Executions, set at the time of Charles I, featuring as head executioner Dennis of the Lillees (after cricketer Dennis Lillee). Careful not to make the show merely a transplanted version of his Australian productions, he filtered Australians out of his studio audience. 'The English people laughed in all the places I thought they should have laughed and one or two places that surprised me.'

Hogan was professional enough to know when to draw the line when taking the mickey out of Britain.

Nobody wants a visitor in their house saying, 'This place is a dump. What awful furniture!' But if they had an ugly painting hangin' up, you'd say, 'That's pretty nice,' and send it up in a mild way . . . The Poms know you can't do a Dubbo [foolish person] if you are one. You can't act stupidly if you're stupid.

What irked him at times was an attitude in Britain that still had about it the air of the Empire, a suggestion that upstarts from the colonies had little to offer. It may not have been a widespread belief but it was held by a few people in important positions.

When I've been in Britain I've found that a couple of people tended to treat me as though I was not mentally very bright because I was an Australian. I'd sit there and think, 'I can buy and sell you in every facet of life but, because I don't talk like you talk, to you I sound like a dumbo.' They had this slightly superior air but I'd soon put a stop to that by saying: 'Listen, fella, I'm richer than you, I'm smarter than you, I'm better-looking than you. Socially, economically and physically I'm superior to you.' Aussies aren't ashamed of their accents any more. Our rock bands have developed their own kind of music instead of simply copying England and America and it is OK to be an Australian.

He added: 'Some London newspapers came out with "Hogan buckets Poms", all about how I supposedly hated the British, which is

Enjoying the English summer on a typical British beach during a break from shooting a television show.

rubbish. I've never been a Pommy-basher and I've never said anythin' like that.'

Of course, before his shows went on air Hogan was fairly well known in the London area through his television commercials for Foster's lager, yet another instance of the advertising industry furthering his show business career. Ten years earlier it had worked in Australia with Winfield cigarettes; now it was happening in England. Until Hogan promoted Foster's, the beer was known in only a few London pubs, introduced in response to the demands of homesick Australians who wouldn't drink the local brews on the grounds that they tasted like they'd been drunk before. Australians had been raised on a German-style lager served cold, often icy, and could not stomach the warm, flat ales of Britain. Londoners began sampling it, found it to their taste and wondered how it had remained hidden all their drinking lives. The manufacturers, Carlton and United Breweries, believed Foster's had the appeal to become a world beer, in much the same way that the Danish Carlsberg was available in the bars of most civilized countries. How to sell Foster's throughout Britain was the problem. The conventional wisdom had been that the European origins of lager should be emphasized. 'We came to the conclusion that the European thing had been overdone, with the profusion of brands with names beginning with "Hof" and "Heidel",' said Dennis Miller, brands marketing director for Watney Mann and Truman, who brewed Foster's under licence. 'We decided we had to so something different and Australian lager was identified as a great opportunity.'

Another selling point was that Australians were known as a race which understood beer. 'The British believe that Australians are credible, and incredible, when it comes to drinking,' said Peter Watkins, who handled the advertising account for Castlemaine XXXX, an Australian rival to Foster's. So that's how far Australia had come in British eyes in 200 years: the writers, artists, musicians, actors, scientists all forgotten under the froth of beer, the achievements of two centuries down the throats with a belch and the request, 'Same again, luv.' The cries of dismay from Australia

Hogan keeps the customers satisfied in a UK ad for the golden throat-charmer.

House could be heard down the Strand, but they were soon to be drowned by the jingle of cash registers in the 12,000 retail outlets of Watney Mann and Truman.

Foster's was launched in 1982 with Hogan spearheading the campaign. Again he was the ocker, not one clad in short, singlet and boots, but an Australian abroad often bemused by the activity around him. ('They know he's not a dope, only pretending.') One commercial showed him in a box at the Royal Opera House, Covent Garden, watching *Swan Lake*, a can of beer in one hand. A male dancer came

on stage. A shocked Hogan put his hand over the eyes of his beautiful female companion, exclaiming: 'Strewth, that fella's got no strides on!'

The advertisements were all good-natured jibes at aspects of British society, small reminders that Britain and Australia, although having much in common, were a world apart. One had Hogan watching British foxhunters in full cry, pointing out that back in Australia there was nothing like a can of Foster's after a hard day hunting dingoes. Then, looking at the baying foxhounds, he remarked: 'Don't think they'll have much trouble catching that funny-looking pack of dingoes.' Another had him standing outside a London pub in a downpour, explaining that Australians cele-

127

With the Prince and Princess of Wales after a performance at the Melbourne Concert Hall in 1983.

brate the breaking of a drought with a can or two of Fosters. 'You too can enjoy Foster's . . . now the drought's broken.' His description of Foster's – 'It tastes like an angel crying on yer tongue' – was so effective that the brand began selling as if prohibition was about to be declared. In the first eight months of the campaign in London, it took six per cent of the capital's lager market at a time when sales of traditional brews were falling; distribution was extended as far as Scotland and a second production plant was opened well before schedule.

Hogan put more than just his face into the commercials. He rewrote some of the campaign because, he claimed later, the advertising agency's copy would have embarrassed Australians with its over-the-top view of the ocker abroad. 'There were certain things in the campaign he thought were going a bit ocker

and he changed them so Foster's was portrayed as being humorous yet sensible,' said Nick Gibbons, Watney Mann and Truman's marketing manager.

Not only did Hogan sell Foster's; ironically, he helped Castlemaine XXXX get a toe in the door, if only because he made Australian lager acceptable. XXXX is made by the Bond Corporation, headed by Alan Bond, of Perth, who aspires to be Australia's biggest industrialist, Foster's by Elders IXL, run by Melbourne businessman John Elliott, who aspires to be Australia's next Liberal prime minister. Deadly rivals in the grand, old-fashioned sense, they rejoice in putting something over on the other. During the America's Cup contest in Fremantle in 1987, largely sponsored by Swan lager, another of Bond's products, Foster's gleefully put up huge billboards around the harbour and kept an extremely high profile. XXXX gained a slice of the British market with millions of dollars spent on advertising the bald statement: 'Australians wouldn't give a XXXX for any other beer.'

Everything was going well for Hogan. In 1983 he performed before the Prince and Princess of Wales at the Melbourne Concert Hall. Three years earlier he had starred in a royal charity performance attended by the Queen and had invited her home, saying she didn't need to get dressed up. After the Melbourne performance he talked backstage with Prince Charles and Princess Diana but wouldn't reveal what was said. 'Of course, I can't tell you too much about what they said, y'know, because there is a pact between me and them. The Queen doesn't go back to England and tell everyone what I said. And I know these two won't either.'

The following year he told British reporters that his show had become a favourite of the royal family. 'Ever since they started screening my show in the UK it's become well known you can't get the royals out on a Friday night. It's a standin' rule – no official engagements because they want to catch the show. And they do the whole bit while it's on, y'know, a can of Foster's, a barbecue and corks danglin' from their coronets.' (Perhaps it should be pointed out that the traditional image of an Australian swagman, or tramp, is one of a character wearing a wide-brimmed hat from which corks dangle on pieces of string to keep the flies away from the face. Furthermore, it works.)

Hogan got on especially well with Prince Charles. After the British screening of the television mini-series *Anzacs*, in which Hogan appeared as an Australian soldier, he had dinner with Charles and Diana. 'Charles told me he had enjoyed *Anzacs*. I pointed out that it had given the Poms a bad time, but he said, "Only the upper-class ones." He's a frustrated comic and we always talk about comedy.'

The easy way Hogan mixed with different strata of society was in contrast to his larrikin predecessor Roy Rene, who was almost sick with apprehension when he had a luncheon date, not with royalty but with the titled Laurence Olivier and his wife Vivien Leigh. Fred Parsons, in *A Man Called Mo*, recounted a conversation he had with Rene on the morning of the luncheon.

'How do I address this mug, pal?'

'Which mug, Roy?'

'This Olivier joker. What do I call him?'

A spot of footy with son Brett, then aged sixteen, in 1975.

'Sir Laurence.'

He repeated it a couple of times, and moved away. Soon he was back. 'I call him Sir Olivier, do I, pal?'

'No, Roy – Sir Laurence.'

'That's right – Sir Laurence. Sir Laurence . . . Sir Laurence . . .' He made a pencilled note, and thought for a while. Then: 'How about the sheila?'

'Which sheila?'

'The mug's missus. What do I call her?'

Parsons suggested he called her either Miss Leigh or Lady Olivier.

Rene said: 'Christ Almight, they've got so many bloody names a man will never remember them.'

At this stage of his career, Hogan was under immense pressure. Sometimes the strain showed. One of the reasons was that he had been so successful in his television career that he was expected to provide a winner each time,

Marital bliss: Mr and Mrs Hogan in classic jet-setting style.

not just a show that beat the opposition but one that left it floundering. A strong showing by just one programme could mean the station on which it was screened winning the ratings war not only for the night but also for the week. The three commercial stations in Sydney and Melbourne were at each other's throats most of the time and Hogan was acknowledged as television's most valuable property. Throw in a Hogan show – if, of course, one was available – and the week was won. One newspaper accurately described him as a 'ratings machine'. When rival stations knew he was to appear, for he was not scheduled on a regular basis, they threw in the best they had against him – overseas spectaculars, or expensive new Australian mini-series.

'It seems as if I'm being used as a club,' he said. 'If I get a rating of 37, which normally would cause them to break out the champagne on other channels, I just get nods and glances. Last time I got a 43 and still there weren't any corks popping. I've made a rod for me own back.'

Writing was also becoming more difficult. Most of the hard grind of writing was his, because he still could not find a team of writers who could produce satisfactory material. He explained his writing difficulties to the Sydney *Daily Telegraph*:

You run into that problem of news repeatin' itself as far as minor issues go, things like the cost of livin' or the fuel crisis. Everything crops up each year and everything you look at, you've done before. That's the frustration. Then something comes up, like the Falklands War, which you think will naturally lend itself. But I'm in a position where the subjects have to be timeless. I wrote this show a month ago and it will be at least another three weeks before it goes to air. I'm in the danger area then of sendin' up the Falklands only to find a helicopter goes down with the Queen's son on board and suddenly I'm tasteless. Or it all dies down and I'm out of date . . . There are just some days when writing doesn't happen. I just can't sit down with a blank piece of paper and say to myself that today I'll write a sketch. It usually comes about after having read a paper or watched the news or overheard something. I wrote the new special in three weeks, even though it's been nine months since the last one. I need a deadline. As soon as I'm asked to do a programme and given a time, I'm right. But I make a lot of excuses for myself. If I think the lawn might need mowin' I'll drop the pen and go out and do it. I don't think it's laziness. It's just that writing is a very difficult thing to do . . .

While everything he touched in his professional life seemed to turn to gold, his private life suffered and became a cliché of show-business success. In 1982 Hogan and his wife divorced. The split had been developing for some time as Hogan became more involved in his work, communication broke down and suddenly there was little to talk about except how they should go their separate ways. As they were Catholics, divorce wasn't easy but they decided the rift was so wide there seemed no alternative.

But as this was Hogan, things were done differently. Even his divorce was like no other. There was no squabbling over who would keep what, no arguments over the family silver and the family dog. Such matters were never discussed. Indeed he didn't move out of the family home but stayed with Noelene, mainly for the sake of their five children (then aged from nine to 22). And then he was courting her again as in the early days, taking her to dinner, surprising her with gifts and communicating. Eight months later they decided to remarry, secretly contacting a priest they knew and arranging for a private ceremony in front of a few close friends and their children. Hogan later told Jerry Fetherston for *Woman's Day*:

We knew this priest, who's a ripper bloke. He's the sort of priest you have to queue to get into his sermons, he's that popular . . . So we decided on this Sunday-night surprise party. Just about 20 people, a bit of grog, good food and a good time . . . Well, about 8.30 or so I yelled for a bit of quiet and told them we were getting hitched. 'Yers had better go into the lounge,' I said. 'We're getting married.' They nearly fell into their Foster's when they trooped into the lounge and there was the priest all set up and rearing to go. It was a great moment for us, a great moment for everyone. There wasn't a dry eye in the house. It was a particularly great moment for the kids. Let's face it, it's not every day that five kids get to their parents' wedding . . .

The Catholic Church, of course, had never recognized their divorce. To the Church the wedding was a reaffirmation of their marriage vows. And, oddly, the media which had charted every move by Hogan since he left the Harbour Bridge knew nothing of the divorce and remarriage until six months later. Hogan's friends had stuck loyally with him and whispered not a word.

'Life's not a dress rehearsal.'
Paul Hogan

Australia had a problem. To be truthful Australia had many problems, nearly all stemming from an enormous trade deficit and the low world prices being paid for raw materials. The Lucky Country, as author Donald Horne called it in the 'sixties, had run out of luck and the relatively new Federal Labour Government, under Bob Hawke, was, to borrow an old bush saying, flat out like a lizard drinking, trying to find solutions. An obvious one was to produce more foreign currency and local jobs through tourism, an industry the country had so far refused to take seriously. Tourism was for Singapore and Hong Kong and Britain. If tourists wished to come to Australia, well, good on 'em; if they didn't, so what? It was in the Australian character to look down on employment in the service industries as coolie labour and of course no one would work on the weekends unless paid handsome overtime rates. Weekends were for going to the football or lying on the beach, not being at the beck and call of hotel guests and restaurant patrons, not working for Poms and Yanks, Nips and Krauts.

Why Australians are not keen on working more than 40 hours a week (or a maximum of

38 as the standard is now in most industries) has been the subject of lengthy discussion. Some say it's the climate, others the egalitarian attitude of workers. Hogan had his own theory.

The 'battler' mentality of the Australian working-class man is what's good about the country and what's bad about it. Havin' a go at something, lendin' a hand to your mates, givin' everybody a fair go are what's good. The party times, the reluctance to work, the 'she'll be all right, Jack' attitude that makes Australia a good place for a holiday are what's bad. Now the holiday's over – which is a tragedy, because it was a wonderful place to live in.

At that time most of the overseas tourist promotion was based on the country's diverse and exotic wildlife – kangaroos, koalas and hairy-nosed wombats – unique to Australia because of the continent's geographic isolation from the other great world land masses. Wildlife as a selling point was scorned by Hogan: 'It's a long way to come to visit a zoo.' John Brown, the Federal Minister for Tourism, was aware of the problem. He had been aware when he was Opposition spokesman on the subject and had often discussed it with an Australian advertising agency, Mojo, which put him in touch with Hogan. Mojo had done considerable work for John Cornell, who had been a key figure in establishing World Series cricket.

'They liked what I was talking about, I liked what they were talking about,' said Brown.

We more or less made a pact that if I became minister Hogan would make himself available for a series of advertisements. Being a constant traveller Hogan was appalled at the lack of overseas knowledge of Australia. He thought as an average Australian – and, of course, he is – that he could use his talents to promote the country. He always had it in his mind to do something. He felt he had made a lot of money out of Australia and he wanted to put something back.

John Brown became Minister for Tourism. A former butcher, he soon became known as the Minister for Good Times because his job took him to such coveted sporting events as the Olympic Games and Commonwealth Games and to leading tourist resorts. His first trip overseas in 1984 raised eyebrows in Federal Parliament when it was revealed that it had cost the taxpayer $69,531, including a hire-car bill of $2,907 for a four-day tour in Italy. His reputation for enjoying himself was reinforced when his wife Jan Murray, a publicist, mentioned in a television interview that she made love to her husband in his Parliament House office the day of his ministerial appointment. This was disturbing enough for a Labour government, which believed that parliamentary offices should be used solely for planning ways to win the next election, but Ms Murray added that they had done it on a desk. And – shock! horror! – there was more: 'I left my undies in his permanent head's ashtray,' she admitted casually. Prime Minister Hawke, not known for a puritanical approach to life, was angered and publicly declared her revelation as 'not in good taste'. Others looked at it more practically and concluded that Ms Murray's admissions could help Labour capture the hedonist vote. His sex life apart, Brown knew what he wanted in tourism and went to the Expenditure Review Committee, which included the Federal Treasurer and representatives of Treasury and the Department of Finance, asking for an increase in the $10 million promotion budget. He was promised an extra $1 million, which was like giving a starving man the smell of a cooking dinner. Brown contacted Hogan, who was in London, and Mojo and together they planned an attack on the Expenditure Review Committee to get the budget doubled to $20 million. Hogan made a 20-minute film clip and Brown took it to the committee.

'It was a very controversial move to get the committee to look at a film clip of someone telling gags,' said Brown. 'But it was a very funny piece. In it he told my Cabinet colleagues, "You give Brownie the money and Mojo and I will sell Australia for you. But you've got to change your attitudes. You can't just sit around the woolshed for ever waiting for cardigans to come back into fashion." It worked. I walked out of there with the $20 million.'

Actually there was more to the film clip than that. The politicians and bureaucrats, more used to indecipherable graphs and statistics as

Happy-snaps from Hogan's latest tourism commercial for American television, featuring his former employer (Sydney Harbour Bridge) and the beach.

dry as old bones, sat surprised when Hogan addressed them on film, reminding them the Australian tourist industry employed 375,000 and earned $10 billion, or about six per cent of the gross national product. 'That's about the worst performance of any country in the world, with the possible exception of Greenland. Johnny Brown wants to double our tourist dollars by 1988. We can do that by '85 if we act now . . . First, you unzip your purse . . .'

The purse unzipped, Hogan went before the cameras and filmed the first of several commercials for the American market, initially concentrating on the West Coast. As he had in the past with Winfield and Foster's, he was making himself known through advertising. Again it was a case of good timing and an instinct for the right move. He refused payment for the work on the commercials.

I have a price – and they wouldn't be able to meet it. And I'm not going to work for a small fee and thereby reduce the price I'd charge everyone else around the world who wants to sell something. Doing them for nothing is the best way out of it.

In *The Stump-Jumpers*, Hogan said his fee for an international campaign of that size would have been in seven figures. 'If we'd gone to the government and asked for $4 million to promote Australia, with $1 million of that going to Hoges, they would have thought this was just another cheap agency trying to line its pockets.' Hogan may have faced the world as an ocker comic but away from the spotlight he was an astute businessman, as was Cornell. They knew where the opportunities lay. Hogan was indignant when it was suggested that his ocker image would do little for tourism, would in fact turn some sensitive souls towards other shores. 'He will be the same character who sold Foster's to the Poms. He didn't make Australians cringe, not even the ones who go over there and adopt the English accent and try and pretend they were born there. He's not a fool.'

It will be noted Hogan often spoke of himself as if he was referring to another character – which often he was.

On another occasion he said: 'I got away from the stereotypical Australian, y'know, the beer-guzzling, bar-fightin' idiot who thinks culture's something you find in a carton of yoghurt.' At a travel industry gathering he was scornful of the professional ocker, that is, an Australian of the old Barry McKenzie school.

There are many types of ugly Australians I've met, including some in England who would drink two pints of beer and throw up three. They're all a bit of an embarrassment to us. But the really ugly Australians are the wimps who get on a plane to England and have an Oxford accent before they get off.

One of the advertisements opened with Hogan at Ayers Rock, the huge monolith in the dead heart of Australia. 'America,' he said, 'you look like you need a holiday, a fair dinkum holiday in the land of wonder, the land down under.' The scene changed to a beach. 'Now here's a few things I've got to warn you about. Firstly, you're going to get wet, because the place is surrounded by water. And you're going to have to learn to say "G'day", 'cos everyone says "G'day" in Australia. 'Course, you'll have to get used to some of the local customs' (Hogan is shown eating at an outdoor restaurant) '. . . like getting suntanned in a restaurant and playing football without a helmet' (a quick shot showed Australian-rules footballers in action) '. . . and calling everyone "mate".' Hogan was now in a pub. Then the scene switched to a barbecue, filmed on the lawns of Kirribilli House, the official Sydney residence of the Prime Minister. 'Apart from that, no worries. You'll have the time of your life in Australia, 'cos we talk the same language. Although you lot do have a funny accent. C'mon, say "G'day". I'll slip an extra shrimp on the barbie for you.'

Initially there was some concern because the advertisements took a different line from conventional ones. For instance, they didn't dwell on scenery or even mention the flora and fauna. The koala was no longer the centre of attention. In fact John Brown had much earlier dismissed the koala, because when picked up and cuddled – the obvious purpose of its appealing design – the creature was liable to scratch and piddle, an accusation that outraged those who considered it the closest living thing to a teddy bear. Brown's slandering of the sluggish, tailless, grey arboreal marsupial became so well known that when Pope John Paul II handled one in Brisbane in 1986 the world's media held its breath, waiting hopefully for a stain to appear on the papal vestments. The vigilance went unrewarded.

Discussing the different approach taken by Hogan in the commercials, Alan Morris of Mojo said:

The most peculiar thing he does in the Yankee tourism stuff is the strange warning about coming to Australia. 'You're going to get wet 'cause the place is surrounded by water.' 'You're going to get sunburnt at restaurants, you're going to have to get

used to playing footy without a helmet' – that's not typical 'Come and see beautiful Queensland' advertising. Very rarely do ads warn you . . .

The commercial proved successful beyond the technicolored dreams of advertising executives. Hogan once more proved that when it came to plugging a product he was up there not only with Barnum but with Bailey, too. He, and the Australian government, had one added advantage, in that the campaign could not have been launched at a better time – because the American tourist's pursuit of the exotic was hitting obstacles. Japan was becoming devilishly expensive; in South America, if there were not wars and revolutions, there were rumours of both; bombs were exploding in the cities of Europe almost as frequently as firecrackers at a Chinese parade; most flights in and out of Athens were suspect; a Medi-

Doing a great job for Australian tourism.

terranean cruise could turn from a glossy travel brochure into a James Bond novel; and the Middle East was to be avoided as if it were the breeding ground of the black plague. Only a few countries, it seemed, were free of terror and terrorism. One was Australia, where the natives appeared friendly, the language was comprehensible, the sun shone, the water was drinkable and the exchange rate was extremely favourable, so American tourists took Hogan's advice and travelled Down Under.

The commercials were successful well beyond the hopes of the Australian government. There were many reasons, which John Brown attempted to explain:

Every survey we've done shows that the best image of Australia abroad, our best selling point, was our friendly nature, our offhandedness, our irreverence. Our iconoclastic nature appealed to Americans. We were the happy, friendly, easy-going Australians. Hogan embodies all of these qualities. In fact I'd say he is the quintessential Australian.

Actually the friendliness portrayed in the commercials was something of a confidence trick. Australia is an insular society, its citizens often hostile towards foreigners. People who dismiss southern Europeans as 'wogs' cannot be considered hospitable. Visitors are frequently insulted, especially those who don't speak English. I have seen Japanese unknowingly smile while being abused for not making themselves understood by shop assistants who left school at 15 and wouldn't know how to spell xenophobia, let alone know its meaning. At the Perth Airport bookshop I cringed in embarrassment as a young female assistant turned to a Japanese tourist trying to use his few words of English to buy a map. 'Haven't got time to deal with youse,' she snapped. 'When youse speak proper, let me know.' On the other hand, Australians like Americans because Americans have easily extracted money and live in a desirable land. Australians tolerate the British, are suspicious of Japanese and have little, if any, regard for French and Germans. They might be friendly in Alice Springs or even Perth, but in the major cities of Sydney and Melbourne the citizens are as preoccupied with themselves as those who live in New York or Chicago. They don't spend their time saying 'G'day' to each other. They're not forever having barbecues to which they invite all and sundry. I have been received with more friendliness in Dallas than in Darwin. Admittedly, these are generalizations, but no more so than the statement that all Australians are friendly.

But the commercials worked, which is what counts in the end. When the commercials spread across America, more than 350,000 calls to an advertised toll-free number were received in 33 weeks. The demand for holiday visas jumped by 80 per cent. An understandably jubilant Minister for Good Times said at the beginning of 1987:

It's the biggest industry we have now. We'll have a turnover getting up around $20,000 million this year . . . There's nearly half a million employees, including about 60,000 new jobs in the last two years. In 1983 we had about 120,000 American visitors, in 1988 we estimate there'll be half a million. Before Hogan we were 49th in the holiday preferences of Californians, now we are number one.

In 1986 the advertisements won first prize in the travel and tourism category of the prestigious US Effie Awards, judged on campaign effectiveness rather than just creative standards. So effective were they that some Californian television stations ran them for three weeks without charge because they attracted other advertisements on the same air time.

For his part in rejuvenating the tourist industry, Hogan was awarded the Member of the Order of Australia, one of the highest honours his country could bestow. He was also named by the newspaper The Australian as its Australian of the Year. While pleased with the honours, Hogan explained his reasons for volunteering to become the tourist symbol of Australia, or at least its human form.

I was just embarrassed by our lack of promotion for the place. I was tired of being taken abroad for a Pom . . . I thought, 'A blind man on a galloping horse should be able to see the tourist potential of the place. If we can't sell Australia, we can't sell anything.' To be number one in the US is a bit special because there's about 100 tourism campaigns over there. And all the ads have got waterfalls and beaches. Even Ethiopia can look good. I believe we got over that having a good time is being friendly. We try to get over that having a good time is atmosphere, not scenery. I really do believe that Australians, despite their gruff up-front style, are really very friendly and pretty hospitable people. I'm not what you call fiercely proud about being Australian. In fact, I dislike that flag-waving business. Nowadays the Australian flag is used to sell everything from margarine to shows. In a funny sort of way that kind of thing really shows people are ashamed of the place. It gets rammed down people's throats.

Another honour was that in a survey of public opinion he was voted the most credible personality in Australia, not surprisingly beating the Prime Minister and other politicians. Soon afterwards a different poll named him the most popular man in the country. Hogan could do no wrong.

Soon after the commercials were screened half of California, it seemed, was saying 'G'day' and wanting to put a shrimp on the barbecue. The shrimp, incidentally, is called a prawn in Australia. Alan Drewe, the Australian Tourist Commission's representative in Los Angeles, was reported in *The Bulletin* as saying that 'Valley Girl' talk – for example 'gross', 'groddy to the max' and so on – was being replaced in the teenage *lingua franca* by 'G'day'. He said that when his children went to school they were mobbed by pupils saying 'G'day, g'day, g'day.' Hogan told an American reporter that because of his campaign there were now more Americans 'in Sydney than in Cincinatti . . . Of course, it seems now that a lot of people expect me to be at the airport to greet them . . .'

The reasons for Hogan's success were, of course, deeply analysed by Americans, who enjoy that sort of thing, and the conclusion was reached that not only was Hogan charismatic, funny and good-looking, but he reminded Americans of the way they were before Vietnam, urban tension and street violence. He had them looking at their past through rose-coloured spectacles, seeing only what they wished, and wondering where in the heck it could be purchased. How about the Qantas ticket counter?

After the Californian success, the commercials were screened on the East Coast with another catchy line: 'If somebody asks you where Australia is, just tell 'em it's where the America's Cup is.' He launched them in the New York Yacht Club, a sensitive place in which to make jokes because the club lost the Cup to the Royal Perth Yacht Club in 1983. The defeat of *Liberty* by *Australia II* in the waters off Newport, Rhode Island gave Australia its biggest boost in the United States. Americans knew little about Australia – or the America's Cup, for that matter – before 1983. Suddenly a trophy they had held for 132 years was taken from them and they began thinking there had to be more to Australia than tennis players, golfers and Olivia Newton-John. Some even opened their atlases to find out where it was. The head of the *Australia II* syndicate, Alan Bond, may have owned Swan Breweries, Foster's deadliest rival in Australia and internationally, but that was of no concern to Hogan as he held court in the New York Yacht Club.

'They let any bugger in here now, do they?' Hogan said cheerfully as I walked into the marble room of the yacht club where he sat smiling, a drink in one hand, surrounded by a dozen or so representatives of the New York media. For Hogan to be allowed to use the club for commercial purposes was a coup; that mere journalists like myself could enter the hallowed portals constituted a major revolution. The New York Yacht Club was so snootily selective that by comparison the Conservative Club in London would welcome Neil Kinnock and the masonic lodge would make the Pope a life member. Maybe the club hadn't understood that Hogan's previous job had been as a rigger on a bridge, not as chairman of the company that built it.

Hogan was not allowed to gloat in the trophy room in which the Auld Mug had for so many years been bolted down, but he noted that excavations were in progress on West 44th Street in front of the marble and granite edifice. 'First thing I'd like to do is thank the New York Yacht Club,' he said. 'If there's one thing I really like it's a gracious loser. We got the Cup and the bolts and when I come here today I see you've started to dig up the whole foundations. Fair dinkum, it brought tears to me eyes.'

He told the assembled media he was getting

(Left) 'Nothing better than sitting down to a few rounds of man *versus* hungry white pointer.' (Above) From the UK Foster's ad; (opposite) from the US commercial.

a little weary of 'G'day' being shouted at him everywhere he went in the United States. 'I don't think I've ever heard so many mangled g'days. And over here you have to translate some of the things that come out of your mouth naturally, like "nick off". I had to explain to Merv Griffin that it wasn't naughty nor anything like that.' Keeping his tongue firmly in his cheek, he said that one of the reasons Americans would like Australia was that there was less gravity. 'You get off the plane you're 12 to 14 lbs lighter. If Carl Lewis came down to Australia he'd broadjump 50 or 60 feet.'

Later he was featured on the top-rated American television show *Sixty Minutes*, telling Americans they were too serious, too intense. 'Life's not a dress rehearsal . . . You're more efficient than we are at doing things, but we enjoy doing things. We're not as tightly wound-up.'

After a segment from one of Hogan's shows, in which people of various faiths competed in a religious Olympics, had been played, he was asked if he had picked on the groups only because of the way they dressed. 'With the outfits some of them wear you can see God has got to have a sense of humour,' he said. 'If the gear they are wearin' is what God wants, don't tell me He hasn't got a sense of humour. He's already sent them up.'

Explaining that Australia was a country descended from convicts, he said:

We were convicts, you lot got away. The ones that escaped went to America, and those of us who weren't quick enough off the mark were sent in convict ships out to Australia. We are partners in crime, we were the rabble and the no-hopers, not so much criminals but people who bucked the system. We were the original rebels. America and Australia have that much in common.

After selling Australia to the Americans, it was considered not a bad idea to sell Australia to Australians. The idea was that if Australians stayed at home for their holidays, it would not only mean less money going out of the country but more jobs. In commercials Hogan was pictured lying beside a swimming pool at a resort on Australia's tropical Barrier Reef. 'G'day,' he said. 'You might reckon I'm just lyin' around taking it easy. But right now I'm flat out workin' for me country.' A waitress handed him a drink. 'I've helped give this girl a job,' he said. Again the campaign was successful, with resorts reporting an increase in Australian bookings.

Hogan's next advertising campaign in the United States was for Foster's lager, prompting Tom Naughton, a Chicago writer, to mourn:

My long and satisfying relationship with a previously obscure beer from Australia is about to end. The trendies will invade at any moment . . . Soon countless cans of Foster's will be poured down yuppie gullets. The same crowd that presently mashes little lime wedges on to their Corona bottles will soon be asking bartenders for 'a Foster's, mate.' They'll probably start wearing adorable

This page and opposite: shots from the US commercials which turned millions of Americans into Foster's aficionados.

Aussie safari hats as well. Now I know how people feel when trendies 'discover' their favourite little restaurant.

What Naughton was saying was that although Foster's had been on sale in the United States for twelve years, it was known to only a handful of connoisseurs – and Hogan's reputation as a salesman was already well established. Hogan was confident his advertising campaign would be as successful in the United States as it had been in Britain.

I know I can sell beer. People at home know I drink beer, they can smell it, they know I like it and they say, 'He's a beer drinker and he likes it, so I'll try it.' But if I tried to sell French champagne it would be a different story. They wouldn't believe that and it wouldn't work. And soap powder wouldn't work. People would know I didn't know about washin' powder. No amount of money will make me tell lies.

Foster's was the eighth largest-selling imported beer in a country where 400 brands vied for the drinker's thirst. The leader was Heineken, followed by the Canadian brews Moosehead and Molson, then the Europeans Carlsberg and Lowenbräu and a couple of Mexican beers. Carlton and United Breweries were determined to change the rankings. In selling beer to Americans image was of utmost importance. Americans don't drink imported beers for their taste as much as for the statement the beer makes, which to Australians seemed a funny way to treat the stuff. The only statement beer makes to Australians is, 'How about another?' Explained Martin Johnson, an importer of beer:

I consider imported beer to be a badge people wear. A guy will buy a $3 bottle of Corona as much to be seen with it. It makes a statement – I'm cool. With Dos Equis he may be showing he's going counter to the trend. With Beck's normally a guy is saying he's affluent, that's he's made it. Moosehead has the image of being a party beer.

With the image all-important, Foster's was not brewed in the United States but imported from Australia so that the 'Made in Australia' tag could be seen prominently on the can.

Hogan's beer commercials had worked earlier in Canada, especially in British Columbia where Foster's had taken eight per cent of the market in a few months. In fact it was so successful in British Columbia that supplies ran out and Carling O'Keefe Breweries, the company licensed to produce Foster's, and taken over by Elders IXL, could not brew enough of the old amber fluid. In order to get the commercials on air for the Canadian summer, when beer-drinking was at its most frenzied, the commercials were made quietly in California; the Canadian winter would have left Hogan and the film crew exhaling ice cubes.

At first Canadians had difficulties with Hogan's treatment of the English language. 'Up-front, there were some problems with people understanding him because we're not very used to Australian accents here in Canada,' said Michael Graydon, Foster's brand manager for Carling O'Keefe. 'But once that was broken down and people started to understand the catchlines, everybody started talking about Paul and audiences now are aware of him.' Soon Canadians were saying 'ripper!' and asking for 'a drop of the amber nectar'.

Foster's was launched in the United States in May, 1986, on a day Australian trade officials had successfully convinced Los Angeles Mayor Tom Bradley should be declared Paul Hogan Day. Of course, Los Angeles declares special days the way other cities have tidying-up campaigns. There's even a Snow White Day, for heaven's sake. But it was a nice advertising gimmick and the Foster's flowed and meat pies were consumed at the Hyatt Hotel in downtown Los Angeles as Mayor Bradley's chief of protocol, Bea Lavery, read the proclamation of the day (shown opposite).

After the proclamation, Hogan joked that they had it all wrong. 'They made a blue,' he said. 'They think I'm the Prime Minister. They thought Bob Hawke was the comedian.' Of course they thought nothing of the sort – the average American would look blank if confronted with the name Bob Hawke. But Paul Hogan . . . well, he was the shrimp-on-the-barbie guy, he was *the* Australian.

The American commercials took a different

'Paul Hogan Day' was proclaimed by the mayor of Los Angeles on the day Foster's lager was launched in the US.

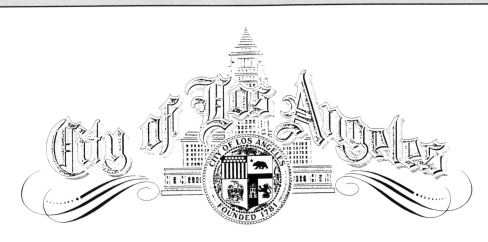

City of Los Angeles

PROCLAMATION

Paul Hogan Day

WHEREAS, PAUL HOGAN HAS BECOME A FAMILIAR FACE TO THE PEOPLE OF THE UNITED STATES AS THE AMBASSADOR OF GOODWILL FROM AUSTRALIA (DOWN UNDER), WHO HAS PROMISED TO "PUT ANOTHER SHRIMP ON THE BARBIE" FOR US IN HIS AUSTRALIAN TOURISM TELEVISION COMMERCIALS; AND

WHEREAS, PAUL HOGAN WILL PRESENTLY EMBARK UPON A NEW TELEVISION ADVERTISING CAMPAIGN IN THE UNITED STATES FOR AUSTRALIA'S LARGEST BREWERY, CARLTON & UNITED, MAKER OF AUSTRALIA'S MOST SUCCESSFUL BEER EXPORT, FOSTER'S LAGER; AND

WHEREAS, PAUL HOGAN'S WORK ON BEHALF OF FOSTER'S LAGER HAS ALREADY AND WILL CONTINUE TO HELP EMPLOY THOUSANDS OF LOS ANGELENOS; AND

WHEREAS, LOS ANGELES SEEKS ALWAYS TO FURTHER AND ENRICH ITS FEELING OF FRIENDSHIP WITH THE PEOPLE OF AUSTRALIA:

NOW, THEREFORE, I, TOM BRADLEY, MAYOR OF THE CITY OF LOS ANGELES, DO HEREBY PROCLAIM APRIL 30, 1986, "PAUL HOGAN DAY" IN LOS ANGELES, AND ON BEHALF OF OUR THREE MILLION CITIZENS EXTEND OUR WARMEST WELCOME TO MR. HOGAN.

APRIL 30, 1986

Tom Bradley
MAYOR

line from those screened in Britain, where he was the innocent abroad. In the United States he gently ribbed Americans, telling tall tales in the tradition of half of Texas and Paul Bunyan, the mythical hero of the lumber camps, whose camp stove covered an acre and had a hot-cake griddle so large it was greased by men who skated on it using sides of bacon for skates.

One commercial had Hogan in a bar telling other drinkers that Australia's favourite sport was shark-wrestling. 'Nothing better than sittin' down to a few rounds of man *versus* white pointer,' he says. When the man beside him shows astonishment, Hogan winks. 'Yeah, course, the hard part is getting the sharks into those tight little wrestling shorts.' Huge posters, bearing a not particularly good likeness of Hogan, went up beside the Los Angeles freeways. Foster's began making inroads into the imported beer market.

Back home Hogan had not been sitting on his backside twiddling his thumbs or counting his money. Although he was no longer producing comedy specials for television, he was looking for other rôles that would fit comfortably. Because he was the most marketable performer in the country, scores of scripts had been sent to him, but he was in no hurry and was certainly not in need of rent money. Hogan and Cornell decided to wait until the right rôle, not almost but precisely the right rôle, came along.

And so it came to pass that into their hands came a script for a £6.5 million television mini-series called *Anzacs*. The story was dear to the heart of Australia, for it was about the blooding of the new nation, about a time of heroes and legends and military madness. The name Anzacs came from the first letters of Australian and New Zealand Army Corps, the men sent to fight World War I, a conflict which was basically European and which, except for the blood ties with Britain, had little to do with a country far off in the South Pacific. After all, the war was sparked by the assassination of two unknown members of the ruling class in a place few Australians knew existed. As the Melbourne newspaper *Labour Call* observed: 'It is unthinkable to believe that because an archduke and his missus were slain by a fanatic, the whole of Europe should

become a seething battlefield . . .' Australia suffered brutally in the war; of the 330,000 Australians who served, 60,000 died and 166,000 were wounded – and that, it should be remembered, was out of a population of five million. They fought first in Gallipoli, in Turkey, landing on a small beach under heavy fire, digging themselves into the steep hills for nine months, then withdrawing, leaving 8,587 dead. Gallipoli was the plan of Winston Churchill, then First Lord of the Admiralty, and it was a disaster. The Australian war historian C.E.W. Bean bitingly said it was caused 'through Churchill's excess of imagination and a layman's ignorance of artillery'.

Then the Anzacs fought in the oozing fields of France and died in their thousands, while old generals quarrelled and talked of honour and tradition. If Gallipoli was a tragedy, the battlegrounds of Passchendaele, Ypres, Fromelles and Pozières were a blasphemy. The Pozières battle was one of the worst of the war. The Germans had developed new artillery techniques, sending shellfire down like a wall through which advancing troops had to move. Day after day the barrages thundered, until the landscape became a wasteland in which bodies were as much a part of the scene as the stark, blasted tree trunks. At times the only way through the barrages was for platoons to hold themselves erect and walk through them. 'It was like waiting for your turn at the hotel bar,' one soldier said. 'Each man was certain to be served in due course.' The history of the 24th Battalion tells of an officer who came upon four soldiers in a trench playing cards. Their sergeant had just been killed during the game and the remainder had picked up his cards and continued the game. When the officer returned all four were dead. In two months the Anzacs suffered 23,000 casualties. Perhaps C.E.W. Bean gave the best glimpse into the savagery of the fighting:

Most men are temporarily half-mad, their pulse pounding at their ears, their mouths dry, the noblest among them are straining their wills to keep a cool head, the less self-controlled are for the time being governed by primitive impulse. With death singing about their ears they will kill till they grow tired of killing. When they have been wracked by machine-gun fire the routing out of enemy

Andrew Clarke (Martin Barrington) and Hogan (Pat Cleary) share a joke off-screen on the *Anzacs* set.

troops is almost inevitably the signal for a butchery of the first few who emerge, and even the helpless wounded may not be spared. It is idle to cry shame upon such incidents unless he cries out upon the whole system of war, for this frenzy is an inevitable condition in desperate fighting. The nobler the leaders, the more they endeavour to mitigate the futile ruthlessness, but ruthlessness is a quality essential in hand-to-hand fighting, and soldiers were deliberately trained to it . . .

The two men responsible for the production of *Anzacs*, the producer Geoff Burrowes and the director and writer John Dixon, wanted to tell individual stories of the men involved, described by the English war correspondent, Phillip Gibbs, in these words:

They were gipsy fellows with none of the gipsy law in their hearts, intolerant of restraint, with no respect for rank or caste unless it carried strength with it, difficult to handle behind the lines, quick-tempered, foul-mouthed and primitive men, but lovable, human, generous souls when their bayonets were not red with blood.

In other words, they were larrikins, but some were more larrikin than others. One such character they devised was Pat Cleary, a man who 'has seen too much and lived too much in the bush to ever feel the need to take life seriously. He lives for the day . . . He is always there when the whips are cracking. Curiously, despite this, he is a survivor. He returns to the bush the way he came down, jumping the rattler but with a wallet that has to be carried in the freight car . . . irreverent, shameless, humorous and irrepressible.' Hogan said that in Cleary he found

a lot of Hoges. He's not a stand-up comic, but he's an amateur pub comedian. Pat's a chook-raffler gone to war, a smalltime hustler. He typifies the Anzac spirit in that he can find humour even in the

Anzacs **gave Hogan his first serious acting rôle, as World War I soldier Pat Cleary, who was able to find humour even in the grimmest of situations.**

worst situations. He's always singin' out in the trenches, slingin' off at the Huns at the wrong time. He was one of those soldiers who kept morale high as scroungers and larrikins. Every unit had one.

When Dixon wrote the character, he had Hogan in mind. But having him in mind and in the series were two different matters. Furthermore the question arose of whether Hogan would be available for 20 weeks. According to John Cribben in *The Making of 'Anzacs'* (1985) Burrowes rang Cornell and suggested he look at the script.

'Sure, we'll always read scripts,' said Cornell. 'But I better warn you we've knocked back the last fifty-two.'

Without a lot of hope but with fingers

crossed, the scripts were sent and a few weeks later Cornell called Burrowes. 'Paul likes the script, mate,' said Cornell. 'Maybe we can get together and have a talk.'

They met at the Melbourne Hilton Hotel. Burrowes talked enthusiastically about the project until Cornell interrupted. 'We've got a bit of a worry. The Yanks have offered Paul a couple of network specials.'

The conditions were as bad for the filming of *Anzacs* as they had been in the battlefields of northern France seventy years earlier.

This was disturbing news. An American network special was the stuff of dreams for most entertainers. They would give their joke book for such an opportunity. But then Cornell went on: 'What we've been thinking is maybe it's a bit early to do network. Maybe we should wait. We reckon Paul should do *Anzacs* instead.'

'You mean you're saying yes?'

'That's about it, mate.'

'Well, bugger me dead!'

The signing of Hogan meant that Burrowes, leaning on the drawing power of the star, could seek more money for his budget, needed to give the series the polish necessary for overseas sales. The budget rose from £6.5 million to $8 million. *Anzacs* was shot at Beveridge, a small town about 50 kilometres north of Melbourne, near where another larrikin, Ned Kelly, was born in 1855. The conditions for filming were foul, cold and wet and the ground gluey with mud, as it had been for the Anzacs. Soon the area was known as Pleurisy Plains because of the biting wind, the incessant rain and the mud in which the company worked. Pumps had to be brought in to reduce the water level in some trenches. A few actors and crew members were ill. On his first day on location Hogan had to jump into a trench sloppy with mud. 'They left out the bit about the mud when they offered me the part,' he said, trying to smile.

There were other problems. A French village had to be built so that it could be destroyed. It rose on a paddock: gabled cottages, the mullioned fronts of shops, rustic buildings with peaked slate roofs and shuttered windows – a replica of a French provincial town at the beginning of the century, totally alien in the Australian countryside. Weapons would have been a problem had the Australian .303 not been so durable. The army was able to supply 300, all in good working condition. The London firm of Baptsy and Company supplied the more exotic weapons, the German Maxim machine-guns and Vickers guns, the Luger and Webley revolvers, and the German Mausers and American Springfield rifles. But a World War I tank proved impossible to find. World War II tanks, yes, we'll deliver one today, sir. Of tanks involved in the first great global conflict there was none, so one was built around the chassis of a D-4 bulldozer, a magnificent machine eight metres long, two-and-a-half metres high and three-and-a-half metres wide. It threw a track on its first day in front of the cameras but was soon performing like a paid-up member of Actors' Equity.

When *Anzacs* was screened, Paul Hogan got favourable reviews but, oddly, from the newspapers and magazines that took themselves seriously, from the same critics who had flailed his comedy on television. The tabloid newspapers were less enthusiastic. Hoges as a soldier whose only job was to kill may have come as a shock, sitting uncomfortably with their perceptions. Later Hogan said the part was not as difficult as he'd first thought. He told *The Bulletin*:

It was certainly nowhere near as challenging as doing an impersonation of Tony Barber or George Negus [two Australian television personalities]. *Anzacs* was to get the viewers used to me in a sustained rôle – accepting me in a rôle where I didn't turn and talk to them every two minutes. I don't think I'd enjoy bein' an actor, hangin' around the set all day to do one line. In *Anzacs* I'd get up and do two lines and duck a bullet and sit around all day waitin' to duck another bullet. I didn't know what to do with meself.

Describing the rôle as similar to playing his grandfather, Hogan said it wasn't a great dramatic challenge. 'I wasn't playing Othello.'

Anzacs was screened in Britain but the United States, perhaps under the impression that no battles were fought without John Wayne, did not rush into the market. *Anzacs* was not bought until *'Crocodile' Dundee* was released, and then only to cash in on Hogan's name. Six hours were cut from the original ten hours on the grounds that the average American 'wouldn't have a clue what "Anzac" stood for'. It was like Australia trimming a movie of the Battle of Little Bighorn so that it didn't show Sitting Bull.

Hogan now felt he could tackle a movie. For years he had received movie scripts but had turned them down for various reasons. But an idea was forming. He had taken a fishing holiday in the Northern Territory of Australia, in many ways still a frontier, had noted the maddening bustle of New York, and wondered how he could bring the two together. As he talked to Territorians while they fished the great rivers of the north, he was struck by the thought that 'these guys, they don't like to go to Darwin – a big racy city as far as they're concerned – and Darwin has a population of about 60,000. If you took a few of those guys and carted them to New York, they would really think they're on another planet.'

The idea grew and he put pencil to paper.

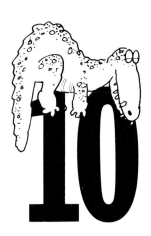

10

'*Movies are fun, but they're not a cure for cancer.*'
Warren Beatty

The crocodile's name was Eric. It was a friendly name for a creature that is one of nature's most ferocious killing machines, a reptile virtually unchanged for at least 60 million years. Eric was about four metres in length and lived in the Kakadu National Park in the Northern Territory, in a stretch of water called the East Alligator River, named in 1820 by British explorer Phillip Parker King. Obviously a better navigator than naturalist, King mistook *Crocodylus porosus* for *Alligator mississipiensis* or possibly *Alligator sinensis*, leaving the river with a name that had no meaning in Australia.

Eric patrolled a part of the river he claimed as his territory, including Cahill's Crossing, a causeway where visitors and residents of the nearby mining town of Jabiru fished for the fat barramundi, one of the most prized fish in Australian waters. The fishermen respected Eric and each time he approached the crossing, then slid over, they scuttled to the river banks until he disappeared. They conceded there was some danger but then they lived in a dangerous area where, it seemed, nature was determined to prove who was in charge and those who intruded should tread carefully lest they tread on their graves. In the nearby ocean were sharks, sea snakes and jellyfish capable of delivering a fatal sting, the bush was the home of venomous snakes and in the rivers, creeks and billabongs lived crocodiles up to five metres in length. So close to nature's deadly arsenal do they live in the Northern Territory that in Nhulunbuy, a mining town about 600 kilometres from Darwin, a crocodile-spotting tower has been built on the beach to help protect bathers. Manned each weekend by members of the Gove Surf Lifesaving Club, it has radio contact with a motorized dinghy, and when one of the reptiles is sighted an alarm is sounded to clear swimmers from the water. The sea wasps, sea snakes and deadly stonefish are the swimmer's responsibility.

In Jabiru, the town built in a wilderness for the Ranger Uranium Mine, devoted to excavating the stuff of doomsday from a landscape barely touched by man, the residents talk at length about the dangers of crocodiles. At the bar of the Sports and Social Club, where the main activity is drinking and no one is admitted unless wearing the minimum dress requirement of shirt, shorts and thongs, the regulars tell tales of crocodiles that attacked aluminium dinghies, sometimes gnawing at the outboard motors; of how dogs have disappeared in one gulp; of the frightening speed at which the creatures can move on land. Some might tell the tale of old Sweetheart, a five-metre specimen that lived in the Finniss River and for reasons known only to him took a dislike to small boats. In the 1970s Sweetheart attacked at least a dozen dinghies carrying fishermen, biting chunks from the sides, mangling outboard motors and destroying fishing equipment. Sweetheart was accidentally drowned when Northern Territory Conservation Commission rangers tried to move him to less popular waters; he now lies, stuffed, in the Darwin museum, to be admired by visitors including Queen Elizabeth II, who shook her head in disbelief when she saw his jaws. Or they might recall how a Weipa fisherman, Peter Weimas, was shaken so hard by a crocodile that his body broke in two.

'The old croc,' the Jabiru locals will say, ordering another beer, 'don't mess around with him. And never turn your back.' The children are told much the same at school.

Instead of being taught the dangers of taking candy from a stranger, or drugs from anyone, they are warned of the perils of entering water anywhere but at the town swimming pool. Jabiru residents now identify strongly with 'Crocodile' Dundee. 'See that bloke over there?' they say, indicating a paunchy fellow leaning against a Landcruiser, 'He's the *real* "Crocodile" Dundee.' Or they point to a dag supporting the bar beneath the punkahs swinging from the ceiling circulating the thick, humid air. 'He could be "Crocodile" Dundee's father.' And they never turn their backs on a crocodile.

Unfortunately in March, 1987, Kerry McLoughlin turned his back. The 40-year-old from Jabiru was fishing at Cahill's Crossing when Eric slid silently up behind, his jaws closed over the man's head and he was dragged beneath the surface. What turned the attack into newspaper headlines around the world, especially in the United States, was that it was seen by six American tourists who, prompted by Hogan's tourist campaign and *'Crocodile' Dundee*, were holidaying in the Kakadu National Park. They were seeking wildlife and some of the frontier atmosphere of the movie, not the nightmare that unfolded; there was nothing like that in the tourist brochures or the television commercials. McLoughlin was decapitated only 20 kilometres from Magela Creek, where several scenes for *'Crocodile' Dundee* were shot.

Everett Galbraith, of Seattle, was taking pictures when he noticed the man. 'I yelled out, "My God, you've got a croc moving down there,"' recalled Galbraith. 'The man got to the middle, then he lost his footing on the crossing and started swimming. The croc had moved to the crossing and started to move in fast.'

His friend Vernon Scott said: 'We could see it happening. There was this slap in the water and then there was nothing – all still. The croc took him downstream and we all watched. I put up my binoculars and I could see the croc across the river. He had something pink in his mouth.'

Two days before Hogan delivered the opening speech at the 1987 Academy Awards in Los Angeles, an American tourist was eaten alive by a crocodile in a remote area of north-western Australia. Ginger Meadows, a 24-year-old former model from Aspen, Colorado, was aboard a cruiser, *Lady G*, anchored in the Prince Regent River after sailing from Perth. She was standing under a waterfall on the river's edge when the crocodile attacked. To add further horror to the story, the crocodile, about three metres in length, tried to grab her body after it had been recovered by police. Wrapped in a plastic bag and tied to the bow of a small boat, the body was being taken to land when the crocodile leapt from the water and tried to tear it away. The director of the West Australian Tourism Industry Association, Jenny Hodder, was philosophical about the death. 'A bit of real danger and excitement is one of the things people look for when they're sitting in the office thinking about an adventure holiday. They could be saying: "Wow, this is a place where people actually get eaten by crocodiles." '

They certainly do. Since 1985 at least eight people have been killed by the creatures, which originally inhabited a vast area from the Kimberley region in the north-west to Maryborough in Queensland, though nowadays they are rarely found so far south in Queensland. Another species, the freshwater or Johnstone's crocodile, can also be found in the north, but these are harmless, preferring frogs, small fish and crustaceans to humans.

The reason for the sharp increase in fatalities in the last few years is two-fold. One is that humans are now spreading into areas where previously few but Aborigines ventured. The other is that crocodiles have been protected since 1971, which has enabled their numbers to multiply. After World War II their skin became fashionable and they were slaughtered to the point of extinction. Dr Graham Webb, of the Northern Territory Conservation Commission, believes they are no longer an endangered species. 'Far from being fragile, their populations must be regarded as being extremely resilient,' he said in an article in the magazine *Australian Natural History* (1986).

In the Territory they are common again. We estimate that before extensive hunting began [in 1945] there were about 100,000 crocs in the Territory. Now the population is back to about half of that, and although the average size of the crocodiles is relatively small, it is growing each year. Because the Queensland Government has not guarded the crocodiles as closely as the Northern Territory has, the numbers there would be far smaller, probably fewer than 20,000.

When Hogan and Ken Shadie began working on the script for 'Crocodile' Dundee they studied the legends and lore of the reptiles; they knew their agility and killing ability. A hero able to survive a crocodile attack and laugh about it later, as did Mick Dundee, was a hero the world needed. They noted that the creature killed its prey by dragging it underwater to drown. Large prey, not necessarily dead, was often dismembered, the crocodile gripping a limb then rolling and twisting the prey around. 'It's a horrific way to die,' said Dr Webb. 'The croc grabs, then tears and thrashes its prey, tearing away chunks of flesh.'

Lying submerged with only the nostril and the eyes, blood-red in the glare of a spotlight at night, above water, the crocodile is difficult to see, unlike a shark whose dorsal fin can provide an early warning. In 1985, Beryl Wruck, 42, decided to cool off late at night in a creek flowing into the Daintree River, North Queensland.

'There was a big splash and Beryl disappeared,' said her friend Serna Mealing, who was only a metre away. 'The last I saw of her was her hands above her head. There was no sound. She disappeared so suddenly.'

In 1986 Kate McQuarrie, 31, was working as a deckhand on a fishing trawler operating out of Karumba, North Queensland. The outboard motor on her dinghy, from which she had been setting nets, broke down, forcing her to swim to the moored trawler.

'I heard a scream, looked around and saw a crocodile with its jaw around Kate,' said the trawler skipper, Robert McNeil. 'Both Kate and the croc disappeared under the water. The attack lasted no longer than 90 seconds or two minutes. I ran inside and got my gun and shot at the croc but the shot misfired, so I fired another shot. Even if the gun had fired correctly I don't think I could have saved her. It was too late by that time.'

In 1986 Lee McLeod, 39, went to sleep on

153

the banks of the McArthur River, near the township of Borroloola, Northern Territory. He disappeared during the night and three days later his putrefied legs were found floating in the river; his torso was later recovered from the stomach of a 2.5-metre crocodile shot by locals.

Even pet crocodiles – and there are those eccentric enough to believe they make agreeable pets – should be treated like a hand grenade with the pin drawn. Alf Casey, a 69-year-old sugar-cane farmer near the North Queensland town of Proserpine, kept a two-metre crocodile called Charlene in his backyard, at times taking her to the local hotel where she sat at the bar with other drinkers, scaring the hell out of tourists and providing fine entertainment for local residents. In 1986 the laughing stopped when Charlene chewed on Casey's left hand while he was feeding her, necessitating amputation of part of the limb.

'She is very docile,' said Casey later. 'It was my own stupid fault I got caught.' However, he received some benefit from the attack. After 'Crocodile' Dundee was released in the United States, the New York television station WNYW5, part of the Fox Network, flew Casey and his wife to New York, taking them to some of the spots shown in the movie and installing them in the Plaza Hotel where Mick Dundee had so much trouble with the bidet. After the attack, Charlene was taken by the National Parks and Wildlife Service and placed on a crocodile farm for breeding. 'I want her back, I'm quite upset,' complained the now one-handed Casey. 'The attack wasn't her fault. I've got visiting rights to see her but I want her back home.'

Although crocodiles are protected by law (slaughtering them incurs a penalty of $2,000 or six months' jail, or both), they are often killed after a human has been taken. After Beryl Wruck was eaten, at least 50 crocodiles were killed by friends and neighbours seeking revenge, none apparently capable of understanding that the creature was merely performing its natural survival functions. Charlie Tanner, a local who has kept crocodiles in captivity for 20 years, was disgusted by the slaughter. 'Boats were going up and down the river every night and they shot at anything in

sight. Nothing was done to stop it. Because a few bloody halfwits get into trouble, you've got this move towards a massacre. All it needs is for a child to be killed and the outcry will be so huge they'll be wiped out – and that's going to happen sooner or later.'

Dr Tony Press, in charge of crocodile management in the Kakadu National Park, pointed out that the reptiles didn't attack humans for the fun of it; it was not an afternoon's sport for them. 'If it was there'd be a lot more people dead,' he said. 'But they attack if they feel threatened and a human is large enough to make them feel that way.'

Warnings are placed throughout the national parks, telling people to keep out of the water, but like speed-limit signs on roads and health warnings on cigarette packets they are ignored, as are detailed warnings in tourist brochures. With a little common sense, fatalities can be avoided, as Jeanette Covaceveitch, curator of reptiles at the Queensland Museum, has emphasized. 'Crocs are very much a part of northern Australia and people who are silly enough to swim where they are do so at their own risk . . . We'd be much more favourable to them than a barramundi would be. Stomach contents in large specimens over the last decade indicate a large proportion of pig bones rather than fish, and there is little doubt they prefer red meat.'

Hogan himself saw the thoughtless stupidity of tourists when during the shooting of 'Crocodile' Dundee he drove a four-wheel-drive vehicle along an outback road. In front was a tourist's car, containing a man and his wife. Arriving at a ford across a river, where crocodile warning signs were prominently displayed, Hogan watched in amazement as the man got his wife to walk in water up to her waist, to ensure the car could cross.

On the other side of the river, Hogan drew alongside the car and gave the driver an earful. 'You'd have to be some sort of a lunatic to let your wife go into a croc-infested river,' he hollered. 'Can't you read the bloody signs?' The man was about to let loose with a colourful reply, when he saw who was driving the vehicle, blinked, shook his head and his jaw dropped. Out here, out in the middle of nowhere, he was being abused by the best-

'G'day': Dundee and friend pay a visit to their local boozer in *'Crocodile' Dundee*. In real life, people have done the same with live crocs kept as 'pets'.

known figure in Australia. Hogan drove off leaving the man speechless.

The Aboriginal people have no difficulty living with crocodiles and have done so for 30,000 years, perhaps longer. To them the crocodile is a sacred creature, part of their magical dreamtime. For some tribes in northern Australia the crocodile is a symbol of the spirit of the place, of new life. In the dreamtime, the crocodile mated with a woman to produce the rainbow serpent, an important mythical creature determining fertility in nature and in the people. The revenge killings of crocodiles saddened Gallarrwuy Yunupingu, chairman of the Aboriginal Northern Land Council.

It is natural for many people to feel like killing a crocodile that has killed a human being. But it is every bit as natural for a crocodile to kill a human being who has wandered into that particular crocodile's territory. . . . Aboriginal people and crocodiles have lived together in this country for thousands of years with a mutual respect of each other's danger. We have killed crocodiles, but only to eat their flesh. Aboriginal people also eat crocodile eggs. But we don't kill crocodiles because they have been in a particular place, or for revenge or 'sport'. All people should have a respect for other animals on earth. We want to live and die the same way, and share this place. There should be no dominating influence. There is lots of room for us to share the country. We've never considered crocodiles as evil things like non-Aboriginal people too often do. We know they're dangerous, we respect them because of that. We walk away from them or around them . . .

The crocodile is a very important part of the life of my people – the Gumatj clan – around Nhulunbuy, because it contains the living spirits of our ancestors. It is our totem, a life- and land-giver, and we believe our spirit becomes a crocodile once we die and leave our bodies. I see the crocodile as part of me. I belong to him and he belongs to me. I cannot educate other people to think like me but at least people should try and see things from the crocodile point of view. Non-Aboriginal people need to respect that fact and not want to shoot crocodiles because a human being has made a mistake and intruded on the crocodile's life.

It's a nice philosophy but not one likely to penetrate the skull of a man with a high-powered rifle and an inferiority complex.

In 'Crocodile' Dundee, the reason why the New York reporter seeks out the hero is that he has survived a crocodile attack, crawling badly mauled back to civilization. It made him a man whose courage was to be admired, a tower of masculine strength in a world populated by wimps, a macho man fighting fabulous monsters like a Homeric hero. Ironically, it was a woman whose real-life ordeal came closest to that undergone by the fictional Mick Dundee. Her name was Val Plumwood. In 1985 she was aged 38, a lecturer in environmental philosophy at Macquarie University, Sydney, when she went alone to the Kakadu National Park to carry out research. In the late afternoon she paddled her canoe through a paperbark swamp on the East Alligator River, a heavy downpour of rain restricting visibility. Through the gloom she saw what looked like a piece of driftwood, then, coming closer, realized it was a crocodile, a large specimen of about 4.5 metres, as she soon found.

The crocodile attacked, lashing the canoe with its tail. Plumwood paddled furiously to the riverbank, then stood in the canoe holding on to the overhanging branches of paperbark trees ready to scramble upwards if the crocodile moved in for the kill. The creature lunged and Plumwood later recalled 'those beautiful flecked, golden eyes'. Plumwood jumped on to the first branch, but not quickly enough; the crocodile's jaws snapped over her left leg, dragging her into water about four feet deep. Getting a better grip on her thigh, the crocodile three times took her into a death roll and when it stopped she somehow got her head above water and clutched the stem of a fresh-water mangrove. Once more the crocodile changed its grip on her flesh, enabling Plumwood to swim away and dodge around the back of a tree, which she then began climing. But again the crocodile was on her, tossing her into the water and swirling her around. Her weakening fingers found the mangrove stem and when the crocodile once more tried to change its grip she dragged herself away.

I tried to get myself up the bank but I couldn't. It was very muddy . . . and I kept slithering down while the crocodile waited at the bottom. I just lay there for a minute thinking I couldn't do any more . . . it would just have to take me and finish me off. Then I discovered I could pull myself up the bank if I dug my fingers into the mud. I got almost to the top when I slid about two-thirds of the way back down and the crocodile was down at the bottom. I got to the top of the bank. To my astonishment the crocodile didn't follow.

Staggering away from the river, Plumwood found her left leg was ripped open halfway around the thigh. She could see the muscle. Using her singlet as a tourniquet and her raincoat as a bulky bandage, she half-crawled through the sodden bush knowing there was no one to hear her cries. For four hours she struggled, often on the verge of blacking out because of loss of blood, until she was found by park rangers two kilometres from where she was attacked. After recovering from her injuries, she was angered to find the crocodile had been hunted and killed. 'You simply cannot create a world removed of all risks,' she said. 'If we did, what kind of a world would it be?'

Another tale that has gone into crocodile legend also involved a female. Her name was Peta-Lynne Mann and in 1981 she was holidaying on her parents' safari camp, which lay 198 kilometres south of Darwin, near where the Daly River ends its long and meandering journey to the Timor Sea, a place of fat barramundi, dangerous boar, wild buffalo and crocodiles. Peta-Lynne and Graham Hilton, a 23-year-old employee at the camp, took an airboat through the swamps and lagoons to see the wildlife, perhaps one of the crocodiles that can weigh 500 kilograms and snap a person's thigh as if it were rotten wood. Ten metres from land, in a swamp of dark, unknown water, Hilton leaned over the side of the boat to recover an anchor rope. His pistol fell from its holster into the water. Unthinking, he dived into the water to search for the weapon and didn't see the crocodile until its jaws were around his left arm. What followed was a terrifying wrestling match, the crocodile dragging one arm, Peta-Lynne hauling on his other. The crocodile let go, allowing the pair to struggle towards the shore, but came at Hilton again, ripping a chunk of flesh about the size of a man's fist from his right buttock. It snapped again and again as Peta-Lynne dragged him through the murky, blood-foamed water, at last getting him on to the bank. Because Hilton's injuries were too severe for him even to think of driving, she had to take their four-wheel vehicle over rough country to the safari camp, even though she had had little experience behind the wheel. Peta-Lynne was twelve years old.

Of course people eat more crocodiles than the other way round. Three crocodile farms in the Northern Territory breed them for the skins and flesh, and great little breeders they are too. The female lays about 60 eggs from October to May, the wet and early dry seasons.

The character of Mick Dundee, bush philosopher and croc wrestler, was based very much on Hogan's own.

Several restaurants in Queensland and the Territory feature crocodile on the menu, which tastes like a mixture of fish, chicken and pork, fairly chewy and not too fatty. The raw meat is white, and is cut from the lower back and parts of the leg and belly. An old bush recipe says that cooking a crocodile is easy. Two pots of boiling water are needed, one for the crocodile and one for a rock. By the time the rock is tender the crocodile will be cooked. This is a bush exaggeration because the meat cooks well if it is prepared carefully.

It has often been said that the people of the Northern Territory are different and if proof were needed it can be found after a fatal crocodile attack. Territorians are almost jubilant when someone is taken. David Nason, of the *Northern Territory News*, explained after a recent attack:

Many Territorians did not feel the horror, remorse or anger that is the normal reaction to violent death. Instead, there was a widespread and bizarre delight in the fact that the crocodile had triumphed. Why this ghoulishness? The answer lies in

the way Territorians see themselves – as rugged frontiersmen carving out an existence in an untamed wilderness. The fact that the victim was a Territorian and not a southern or overseas tourist seemed to make little difference. It was as though an occasional croc victim was needed to reinforce the cult of Territorianism.

So much do the people of the Northern Territory like their crocodiles, they are building a hotel in Kakadu National Park in the shape of the reptile. In this $12 million example of kitsch, guests will be able to stay in the crocodile's body; the head will be the foyer, the tail will be staff quarters, and the legs will be parking lots. The central area will be open, displaying what passes for the beast's alimentary canal, and its heart will be the swimming pool. Presumably crocodile steaks will be on the menu.

But even though the crocodile has become the symbol of the north, it hasn't stopped poaching. The skins are worth $400 or $500 and they are not a difficult beast to shoot, not when caught in a spotlight at night. 'Crocodile' Dundee was not only a 'dynamite fisherman', that is, one who uses explosives to stun fish so that they float to the surface (an activity frowned upon by authorities), but was also not above a little poaching of the protected species. This brought a stern rebuke from Dr R.G. Vorlicek, a member of a team of researchers at Sydney University's School of Physics which monitors saltwater crocodile populations. 'It is unfortunate that humour would appear to be derived from the illegal killing of a protected species,' he said. 'One wonders if there would have been quite as many sniggers if the "fisherman" had been after koalas or baby fur seals.' Unfortunately for the crocodile it is not a creature one yearns to cuddle.

Leaning on these stories, Hogan prepared his script, writing in longhand in pencil. 'It's common sense,' he explained when he was asked why he didn't use a more modern method. 'I knew there'd have to be four or five drafts. No first script is written in stone.' Added an admiring Cornell: 'We didn't need to change a word of some characters . . .'

Since 1974 Hogan and Cornell had been offered movie scripts, the first of them *Don's Party*, adapted from the David Williamson play about an election-night party. But even then Hogan was thinking of borders beyond Australia and rejected *Don's Party* on the grounds that it would not travel overseas. More scripts came in, especially when Hogan found a certain fame in America through his tourist commercials. Some were from the big studios, others from entrepreneurs who saw the potential of the former bridge rigger. One was for a television series called *Yank and Dink*, described as a sort of *A-Team* that co-starred an Australian. No thanks! Hogan was interested in the big screen because he was continually frustrated by the confines of television. As he put it:

Television's fine, but you've never got the time or the money. If you want to do *Custer's Last Stand* on television you've got to use three Indians. Four you can't afford . . . On television every sketch you write ends up being a compromise of some sort – they say you can't have fourteen people because it's too expensive, that sort of thing. I think writin' comedy for a movie is actually easier because you create a certain reality. On the television shows I might get dressed up as a copper and fall down some stairs. Now if I really was a copper and I fell down some stairs it would be hilarious, but the viewers know it's just Hoges dressed up and in a few more minutes I'll be back to being me. See, in a movie you have the time to bring the characters to life . . .

Despairing of finding the right script, Hogan thought he might as well do it himself. He recalled New York and how it was the absolute opposite of the Northern Territory. New Yorkers thought he was funny so he reckoned they would split their sides laughing at some of the outback characters he had met in the Territory. And then there was the fish-out-of-water concept that appealed, a theme used countless times but one that could always be polished and represented. Furthermore he wanted to create a new Australian hero because he didn't have a high opinion of those who had previously been presented to the public. He explained to John Baxter for *Cinema Papers*:

There's a lot about Dundee that we all think we're like; but we're not, because we live in Sydney. He's a mythical outback Australian who does exist in

Though Cornell (left) is not Hogan's Svengali, he oversees contracts, finances and Hogan's image.

part – the frontiersman who walks through the bush, picking up snakes and throwing them aside, living off the land, who can ride horses and chop down trees and has that simple, friendly, laid-back philosophy. It's like the image Americans have of us, so why not give them one? The Americans have been creating folk heroes for years. They made folk heroes out of villains: Billy the Kid was a grotesque, deranged 16-year-old who went around shooting people in the back with a shotgun. When they made the movie Paul Newman played the part. But we've always been desperately short of folk heroes in this country. Ned Kelly is pathetic. [He told another interviewer Ned Kelly was 'a half-wit Irish bankrobber, who used to rob banks with a bucket over his head, unsuccessfully.'] So are the bushrangers. So, I thought, I'll make up one, a typical modern-day outback lad, and set him loose in New York.

He thought about other personalities from Australia's factual and fictional past and didn't rate them highly, dismissing Peter Lalor, leader of the miners' revolt at the Eureka Stockade, Ballarat, in 1855, revered by many as Australia's first revolutionary, as 'a sort of politician who wrote poetry'. He believed the Banjo Patterson character, the Man From Snowy River, hero of a successful movie and the subject of a second feature which went into production in 1987, was 'pathetic – one bloody ride down a hill.' He had a dig at Phar Lap, the racehorse which is now part of folklore. 'We've got so few heroes a horse figures in our top five.' They were not what he had in mind; what came out as he scrawled in longhand was a hero who would not only overcome the odds but would make people feel good when they left the cinema.

Hogan put down all he knew about crocodiles, all the stories, tall or otherwise, he had heard from the hard men who lived in the outback; when the contrast of New York was added to the adventures down under, and when the character was defined, using not a little of Hogan's own personality, his thoughts turned to financing the project. Cornell had that worked out already, because in matters of business he is the brains in the partnership. Hogan has an instinct for what is the right move but Cornell knows about finance and the small print in contracts. And Cornell is the one who ensures that the Hogan image is not sullied by ostentatious displays of success, that in the public eye Hogan remains the average knockabout bloke even if he is a millionaire. Cornell, for instance, would never agree to Hogan being photographed with his Porsche, a plaything he bought because it was the closest to the motorbikes he had loved when a youth. And when Hogan was seen reading a James Bond paperback in public, Cornell reportedly jumped up in alarm. 'Don't start reading bloody books. You're liable to become literate and ruin the whole thing.' But then he was probably joking. Cornell is not a Svengali; even the suggestion would annoy the usually easy-going Hogan.

Money has never controlled Hogan's life, proved by the fact that early in his career he knocked back a $1 million offer to do a weekly comedy-variety show. 'He thought about it for just a few seconds, then said, "That's not for me," ' said Cornell. Hogan's philosophy was that there was more to life than slogging away all day to please the tax man. 'It would have been a drag, like working in a bank,' Hogan explained. 'I'd rather be able to stay in bed till 9.30 or 10, a nice civilized hour like that, then go to the beach. Money's not the main motivation.'

The way the pair operate can be seen in a story Hogan told of the time Kerry Packer, head of TCN9, was trying to woo him back from a rival television station. 'We went into Kerry Packer's office,' said Hogan, 'and the first thing Kerry says to me is, "G'day, Hoges, do you want to come back to Channel Nine – come back home?" I said just as quickly, "Half a million dollars' transfer fee, Kerry."

'Kerry laughed and said, "I'll talk to your manager. He's probably got a better idea of money than you have."

'He turned to John Cornell and said, "How much, John?" And John said, "Half a million dollars." Kerry laughed. We didn't.'

Movies in Australia can be financed two ways. One is by seeking help from the federal and state film commissions, the way many of the earlier Australian successes were financed, or by going to private investors who can qualify for handsome tax concessions on their investments. 'Crocodile' Dundee was to be private investment, if only for the reason that Hogan had little time for government subsidies. 'Probably the government shouldn't be in the Australian film industry. They clutter up the place half the time. And if an industry's worth persevering with, it should hold itself up.'

Cornell and Hogan had several mates willing to invest, mostly from the sporting arena. Former Australian cricketers Greg Chappell, Dennis Lillee and Rod Marsh put in money. Lillee was the biggest investor with a $50,000 stake, which by the middle of 1987 had returned him around $110,000. Chappel invested $45,000 and Marsh $20,000. About 600 investors contributed an average of $14,400. The minimum investment was $5,000, and the biggest $50,000. The movie's prospectus emphasized Hogan's popularity in the United States and 'that was good enough for me,' as one small investor, Mike Wood, a Sydney management consultant, said.

Hogan was paid $218,000 for the script and $450,000 for starring in the film. He put £440,000 back into the budget and his wife Noelene and their five children invested $10,000 each. Cornell, who was paid $150,000 as producer, invested $250,000.

In the early stages of raising money, Cornell and Hogan realized they didn't have enough capital to do it themselves, which they would have preferred. Cornell ran into an old schoolmate he hadn't seen since he was eleven, Denis Johnston, of the Brisbane broking firm Paul Morgan and Company. They talked about the movie and finding funds.

'I'll get you the money,' said Johnston, and Paul Morgan underwrote the $6.8 million budget. Morgan, also known as Porky, a larrikin in the Hogan mould, who once described himself as 'one of Queensland's most upwardly mobile pisspots', recalled going to see Cornell's accountants to discuss details of the deal. 'They were pretty astonished at our antics and the way we bowled in. You know, they expected us to be nice clean-cut youths, upstanding and all that.'

Morgan himself put in £500,000, which, he calculated soon after, would return him three or four times the amount. Another of Morgan's clients was a businessman who invested $250,000, basically for the tax concession, a profit not being necessary. He is now about $2 milllion better off and his swimming pool features a smiling blow-up crocodile.

So acceptable was the Hogan name, so golden his touch, so accurate his instincts, that there was no shortage of investors.

'When we were raising the funds we sent back a couple of million,' said Cornell. 'We were over-subscribed.' The investors, most of whom were in the top tax bracket of 60 per cent and were therefore anxious to find ways to give the government less, qualified for a 133 per cent tax deduction and the first 33 per cent of profits tax free. Soon afterwards, the government reduced these concessions to 120 per cent and 20 per cent.

Although he had plenty of opportunities, Cornell was not interested in pre-selling the movie, the most popular method of funding. He was determined to do it his own way, as he explained to Mike Harris in *The National Times*:

Most Australian movies try to get a pre-sale. I think that's probably the worst way to do things. It cuts down any chances of having a movie that might make millions. You've done the deal beforehand, and the deal you do beforehand with an unknown quantity is nowhere as good as with a finished product where people can see what's happened and sit down and laugh at it. So I declined all requests for them to read scripts and things like that . . .

Small by American standards, the budget was big enough in Australia to allow Cornell and Hogan to hire the best talent around, such as cinematographer Russell Boyd, who had worked on *Picnic at Hanging Rock*, *Gallipoli*

With co-star Linda Kozlowski. At one time Australian Actors' Equity was insisting that her rôle should be played by an Aussie.

and *Mrs Soffel*, and designer Graham Walker, known for his work on *Mad Max*, which until *'Crocodile' Dundee* was, in financial terms, the most successful Australian-made movie ever. Peter Faiman, the director, had produced Hogan's television specials and several expensive, large-scale productions for the Nine Network, including Royal Command performances and Elton John specials. But he had never directed a movie. John Meillon was signed to play Mick Dundee's partner in Never Never Safaris ('It's called that because if you go on one you'll never, never come back'). A fine character actor who has appeared in 36 movies (including *On the Beach*, starring Gregory Peck, Ava Gardner and Fred Astaire), and a dedicated consumer of beer, Meillon has achieved a certain fame by having a bar in a Sydney hotel named after him.

'I was there so often they thought they might as well make it mine,' said Meillon.

Hogan wrote the part specially for Meillon, if only to stop him asking each time they met: 'Hey, mate, when are you going to get a part for me?' Hogan's son Brett was employed as lighting cameraman.

The important female lead rôle went to Linda Kozlowski, more or less an unknown as far as movies were concerned. She had however made a name appearing with Dustin Hoffman in the Broadway production of *Death of a Salesman* and had appeared in the subsequent movie. 'Dustin Hoffman recommended her to us,' said Hogan. 'We figured, if he doesn't know, who does? He's a reasonable type.'

Kozlowski was not signed without problems. The storyline demanded a New Yorker but Australian Actors' Equity, the trade union for thespians, was not keen to give permission for an actress to be imported, putting forward the usual argument that the rôle should go to an Australian. Hogan thought that ridiculous. Often he had winced when watching an American actor play an Australian, usually by employing a bad English accent. He wasn't going to have that embarrassment in his movie, not when it was aimed at American cinemagoers who would also have winced and probably walked out.

'No way,' he told Actors' Equity. 'We're not wandering around the outback making an Australian telemovie. We'll be on location in New York for six weeks. We're going to be covered by the media while we're there. We'd look absolutely stupid if we said, "Here's our American girl. Of course, she's an Aussie but she does a good accent." ' To emphasize further the importance of the character, Hogan stressed she had to be from New York, not even a Hollywood lady but one wise in the ways of the Big Apple. At one stage Morgan Fairchild was considered, but was rejected, along with a few other big names, on the grounds that she might lock herself for hours in her dressing-room getting motivated before she could light a cigarette. The matter was taken to the National Disputes Committee, which handles situations which producers, or any other importers of talent, and the union cannot agree. In the end, Equity did not bother even sending a representative to the disputes committee, a tacit admission that it did not have a case. There was also a suggestion that Equity thought twice about taking on such a popular figure as Hogan, himself a member of the union.

'Neither Paul Hogan, nor the many other producers Equity has treated with disdain in the past, should have to put up with this abuse of power,' the *Sydney Morning Herald* thundered in an editorial.

The movie was ready to shoot. Hogan had no doubts about his ability to corner a fair share of the market but there were times he allowed himself to ponder on the huge gamble he was taking. 'If this film fails, then I've failed,' he told veteran show-business reporter Matt White. 'Not just as a performer but financially. I've put everything I've worked for into it.'

And so they went forth to make a movie, this unique trio of Faiman, Cornell and Hogan – a director who has never directed a film, a producer who had never produced one and a star who had never starred in anything beyond the confines of television and whose international appeal came largely from commercials. It was so unlikely that maybe one day it will become a movie plot.

'There's too much pretentious nonsense talked about the artistic problems of making pictures. I've never had a goddam artistic problem in my life, never, and I've worked with the best of them.'

John Wayne

Nothing much had ever happened at McKinlay. A hamlet with a population of thirty, it lay on the great, dusty semi-arid plains of north-west Queensland where more than 400 millimetres of rain in one year would be likened to Noah's Flood. To the north was the metropolis of Cloncurry (population: 2,000), to the south the bustling sprawl of Winton (population: 1,300). Winton was the birthplace of Australia's international airline, Qantas, formed in 1920, its name coming from the initials of Queensland and Northern Territory Air Services, not as some may have suspected from a rare species of bird or a marsupial that could fly. A little distance from Winton, at Dagworth station, Banjo Patterson in 1895 wrote 'Waltzing Matilda', the unofficial Australian national anthem and preferred drinking song, especially after midnight; he took his theme from an incident which occurred at Combo waterhole in the Diamantina River. And that's about all there is to be known about the country around McKinlay.

The settlement itself had a wide dusty street and a pub. Perhaps the most excitement ever generated there was the occasional fight on a Saturday night, but mostly the folk of McKinlay got on with the difficult task of making a living from land that was never intended to grow much more than scrub. Then in July, 1985, Paul Hogan and the cast and crew of 'Crocodile' Dundee arrived to shoot the opening scenes of the movie. McKinlay became Walkabout Creek, which was supposed to be much further north, up in the tropics where the crocodiles lay waiting. But no matter – this was the movies, where anything was possible, so the Federal Hotel had its smart aluminium sliding doors removed, a false façade was erected and it became the Walkabout Creek Hotel. The paintwork of the police station was smeared with a dirty grey substance and a vacant shed was transformed into a bush garage.

When 'Crocodile' Dundee was a massive success at the US box office and American tourists were landing on Australian shores as if it were D-day on the beach at Normandy, many visitors inquired about the Walkabout Creek Hotel. 'That cute little place in the movie,' they would say, 'how about we stay there?' Australian tour operators had a difficult time explaining that it didn't exist. Sick of the enquiries and at the same time realizing there was a dollar to be made, the hotel changed its name to the Walkabout Creek Hotel. Hundreds of tourists visited it but all they found was a little country pub, the only connection with 'Crocodile' Dundee being a Never Never Safari Tours sign autographed by cast and crew, movie stills on the wall and a large mural from the film. But something must have worked because in 1987 the owners put the pub on the market for $280,000 – double the price they had paid two years previously. In New York the Plaza Hotel, where Mick Dundee stayed, faced similar problems to the McKinlay pub. In the movie, Dundee could not fathom what a bidet was all about, which made for a couple of amusing scenes. Plaza guests demanded a similar room so they too could be puzzled by a bidet and the hotel staff had to patiently explain that the establishment lacked such interesting accessories, and that the hotel room in the movie was built on a set.

Everyone has a different attitude to the outback. For many Australians living in cities, it fills their dreams and they declare that one day they will hitch a caravan to their car and drive the long, lonely roads to discover it for themselves. Some do. Many are disappointed, for it can be an uncomfortable place of heat and dust and monotonous landscapes shimmering into a horizon that is never reached. You can pass a whole day without seeing another person on the road, or even a house, or the slightest sign of civilization. And when night falls and the travellers are grimed with red dust, their throats are parched and all they've seen is a dead snake on the road, the glamour, the dream, wears thin.

John Meillon admitted that the outback wasn't his favourite place.

I endure the outback, I don't enjoy it. I remember the day we were in some outback town and we all came out and stood on the hotel verandah and looked at each other. And we looked at one another again. There was absolutely nothing to do. I walked around the hotel and came back to the verandah and everyone was still standing there. So I went into town and the only thing open was the vet's office. The vet said, 'Can I help you?' and I said I just wanted a chat. 'Oh,' he said, 'in that case I'm closed.'

While the locals welcomed the money brought into McKinlay by the movie, at times they became vexed over the unusual activity, especially by the way a movie company tends to take over a small town. A movie company does not merely set up cameras and shoot. It orders people off the street, stops traffic, silences anyone talking above a whisper and generally disrupts the day-to-day life of a community. The excitement put goats off their milk, hens used as props went missing and cars had to be parked off the street in backyards. 'It's no credit they chose McKinlay for their film. They only came here because the town was on its uppers,' said a local, Jack Hardy, meaning that McKinlay was not wallowing in wealth.

'Crocodile' Dundee was shot the way the story unfolded, first in Australia then in New York. McKinlay was the place where Mick Dundee's rowdy friends drank on into the

As it said on the film posters, where Mick parts the Manhattan skyscrapers: 'There's a little of him in all of us.'

night, where New York reporter Sue Charlton looked around at the boozing and brawling and wondered if she should have stayed home. It should be pointed out that such characters are not exaggerated. In parts of the outback, where there are few women, 'a fight's as good as a fuck', to use a vulgar old expression.

A brawl does not mean that the combatants are enemies, rather that they're friends letting off steam and entertaining themselves, for these are places where there is no television, no cinema, no local hall to accommodate a passing Shakespearean company, or even a country singer, nothing but booze and each other to pass the hours. In some bush hotels the patrons engage in what they call bullfights. With heads lowered, they charge each other, their skulls colliding with a sickening thud; the last man on his feet is rewarded with many glasses of beer.

I've seen the brawls, and avoided the fists, when travelling in the outback with an old friend, Larry Dulhunty, who ran a boxing tent which also featured singing, whip-cracking and rifle-shooting. We would arrive at a small town during the annual race meeting, the place crammed with hard-drinking stockmen who left their lonely cattle stations only once or twice a year, and the local policeman would greet us with a look of relief. 'Thank God you're here,' he would say. 'Now I can get 'em fighting in your tent.' And when a brawl broke out in the pub, which it did twenty times a day, the pair would be ordered to the tent, always pitched as close as possible to the hotel, to continue their fight, the penalty for not doing so being a ban on buying beer. No penalty was greater! And half the pub drinkers would pour into the tent to watch the fight, for which they were each charged the not unreasonable sum of $2. And not only the men were tough. Some women in the outback could handle themselves equally as well as the men. One night when Dulhunty was performing in front of an outback audience that had been drinking heavily, he got fed up with the heckling of a woman and started (verbally) abusing her in return. Up jumped a large person, what looked like a giant in the shadowy tent, wearing an old army shirt and tattered football shorts, and began swinging

what could only be described as haymakers. Dulhunty ducked and weaved, looking for an opening, found one and drove his right fist at the giant's head. He knew the punch was well timed because he felt it jar his elbow. The giant staggered back into the audience, blood pouring from a broken nose.

There was a hush in the tent. Then someone yelled: 'Hey! That's a woman you just hit.'

Unbelieving, Dulhunty turned to the local policeman. 'That's right,' he said. 'Things might become ugly, so I reckon you should finish your show and, to save trouble, refund everyone's money.'

Dulhunty made the offer but only six people left and the show went on. Next day he was told that no one thought less of him because he had broken the nose of the woman. 'She's the town bully,' it was explained. 'Only the other day she bashed a shearer over a pool game.'

Dulhunty, to whom I introduced Hogan a decade ago, has been involved in gun battles, been a rodeo rider, been run out of towns and welcomed in others, been a gambler, a pool hustler and a fighter of legend in the outback, once brawling with bare knuckles for three hours in Charters Towers before both men called a halt on the grounds that they were likely to kill each other. He still takes his boxing tent on the road and if necessary will fight himself, with or without gloves. He is over 60 and would fit comfortably in the bar of the Walkabout Creek pub.

Besides fighting, bush people are extremely good at fixing things – almost anything. Give them a screwdriver and a piece of fencing wire and they'll send a stalled battleship on its way, or in Hogan's case a helicopter (and he didn't need the fencing wire). In one of the first shots for 'Crocodile' Dundee, near Cloncurry, the helicopter was required. But the machine would not take off. Something was wrong with the motor.

Several people offered advice. Hogan turned to Meillon and said: 'I'll fix this.'

'You fix it. How?' said Meillon.

'Give me a screwdriver.'

Armed with the necessary tool, Hogan walked to the helicopter and poked in the engine compartment. Soon after the helicopter's blades began turning.

Setting out for a gentle stroll through 'the most hostile and primitive land known to man': Mick and Sue Charlton.

'How'd you do that?' asked Meillon.

'Simple, son, had a screwdriver.' He did not tell anyone until later that the helicopter's motor fired coincidentally as a result of his poking with the screwdriver.

In between shots, Hogan was asked by a reporter if the character of 'Crocodile' Dundee had any similarities to Barry McKenzie. Hogan shuddered. Many Australians shudder when they recall Barry McKenzie, a creation of satirist Barry Humphries which appeared in the British publication *Private Eye*, in the late 'sixties and early 'seventies. Bazza, as he was known, was an ocker of the worst kind, chundering and farting and drinking his way around London, causing no little problem to the many Australians living in Britain who were trying to establish a reputation as reasonably couth persons. Bazza wouldn't let them. There were, of course, numerous Australians who revelled in the character and tried to prove that life imitates art. McKenzie emerged from the *Private Eye* comic strip to appear in two movies, both of which made good profits. All the two characters, Bazza and Mick,

Persuading a road block to step aside: a bush scene from 'Crocodile' Dundee.

shared was an innocence when abroad, a simple approach to life in a complex world.

'Barry McKenzie?' Hogan snorted. 'Not bloody likely. Bazza was obsessed with bodily functions. He was an idiot, an Australian fool for the English to laugh at. My character, "Crocodile" Dundee, is a horse of a different colour. He doesn't make a fool of himself wherever he goes and he's not obsessed by pointing Percy at the porcelain. Dundee may be naive and a larrikin but he's no fool. He'd chew Bazza up and spit him out before breakfast.'

Having established that, the cast and crew moved to Kakadu National Park . . . and back to another time. Hogan summed up Kakadu as well as anyone when he told an American reporter: 'It's the kind of place where, if a pterodactyl flew by, you'd nod and say, "Yeah, that's about right." '

Lying about four hours' drive from Darwin, now a modern city of 60,000 completely rebuilt after being wiped off the map by Cyclone Tracy on Christmas Eve, 1974, the park sprawls over 17,000 square kilometres and is divided into three stages according to its environmental value. Stage one, comprising some 6,144 square kilometres, was listed in 1981 by UNESCO as one of the World Heritage Properties, the first Australian area to be so designated. It is a complex landscape of spectacular escarpments that wind for 200 kilometres, of mangrove swamps, rivers and creeks, lagoons and rock pools, monsoon forest, dry forest, grassland, flood plains and uplands. There are 28,000 species of plants, 10,000 species of insects, 350 different kinds of birds, 60 assorted mammals, ranging from the pale field rat to the water buffalo. The lagoons are covered with the blue, yellow, white and red flowers of lilies, under which crocodiles wait for a passing magpie goose. Across the lily leaves lotus birds stroll on long toes, tucking their eggs or young under their wings, and fleeing if threatened. Ibis, egret and heron swoop in to feed. Dingoes prowl in the night and wallabies graze timidly on the young, sweet grass. In hidden caves and chasms are Aboriginal rock paintings of ancient figures and dreamtime myths, some created 10,000, maybe 20,000, years ago. From the escarpment spectacular waterfalls tumble into gorges.

This was 'Crocodile' Dundee territory . . .

Filming wasn't easy in this remote, rugged area. For one thing, there was no lack of crocodiles and a guard, a .45 strapped to his waist, was hired in case they became too friendly. Delvene Delaney, who was helping her husband Cornell on location, thought for a moment she was going to feature on one's menu. With the camera crew she was in a boat looking for action shots of the reptiles when one about three metres long was spotted lying on a bank. 'Everything seemed to be okay until the croc suddenly took off into the water straight at our boat, with a huge swing of his tail and his mouth gaping open,' she said. 'He was so quick. One second he was there, the next he was heading straight for us.' The boat took off, following a course recommended earlier by Cornell, who by now was an expert on *Crocodylus porosus*. 'The local advice is to zig-zag. Apparently they're not too good on the turns.'

But when the time came to shoot the movie's crocodile scene, in which one launches itself out of the water and almost takes Sue Charlton, the crew moved out of Kakadu. They went to Girraween Lagoon, near Darwin, used previously for crocodile attacks in the popular television melodrama *Return to Eden* – and in the unpopular and expensive saga of early explorers *Burke and Wills*. The lagoon was chosen for the sensible reason that it contained no crocodiles. 'The director was interested in utilizing a real crocodile,' said Mike Atkinson, a Darwin cinematographer hired because of his local knowledge. 'He said we could use a real croc and drug it and in that way you could get realistic movement. But the

insurance companies did not like the idea. They said it wasn't foolproof. So in the end we had to build a mechanical croc and install it on a rail.'

The designer, Graham Walker, revealed:

It cost $45,000. It operated on hydraulic power. Its jaws opened and closed. It could lunge, jump up and down, turn and switch its tail. It was made out of rubber latex. Very realistic. We were fortunate. You see, we were able to take the mould of a skin of a five-metre crocodile. It surged up on rails in the movie and I reckon it looked like the real thing.

After several months of work the crocodile appeared in the movie for about 20 seconds. It was launched at Sue Charlton after crew members had dug 50 square metres of mud from the lagoon so that hydraulic rams could be installed to fire it out of the water.

Walker also designed the Walkabout Safari truck, a battered vehicle covered with grease and dust – admittedly, not as difficult a design as the truck he made for *Mad Max III* which had to run on railway lines and was powered by 'methane gas derived from the poop of 400 pigs', but still a fairly unsavoury form of transport.

The crocodile scene resulted in Hogan's first screen kiss, an occasion awaited eagerly by the tabloid press, not to mention the film crew, whose members stood around offering advice and rude comments. 'Calm down, Hoges,' they called as he went in for the clinch. He did it in three or four takes to the applause of the crew. 'No, I wasn't embarrassed,' he said later. 'I'm too long in the tooth to blush. Besides, I'm a good kisser.'

There were, of course, no hotels for cast and crew at Kakadu. They took over Ja Ja Camp, a collection of huts and portables owned by the Pancontinental mining company. Some slept under the stars. 'Look here,' said Lee Dillow, Hogan's personal assistant, 'this is not good enough. Too much dust and not enough sheilas. When we do the sequel, let's call it 'Mudcrab' Dundee so we can hang around Noosa for a while.' He was referring to a luxury tourist resort on the Queensland coast where the delectable mudcrab lives in mangrove swamps and dies in restaurants.

Still, the camp was made as comfortable as

possible. Cornell supplied the beer, which meant interesting nights around the campfire telling lies and singing. On the final night in the Northern Territory he served Veuve Clicquot champagne, which, out there under the stars in a primitive crocodile-infested landscape, made him arguably the most popular producer in the history of the cinema.

Some of the scenes were shot at UDP Falls, an idyllic location except for the name, which translates jarringly as Uranium Development Properties. Near the area were yellow 'Keep Out' signs warning of radioactive uranium tailings. 'Didn't take us long to bugger up the place,' someone observed. The waters around the falls were home to crocodiles but they were of the harmless freshwater variety. Cornell, also an authority on *Crocodylus johnstoni*, reassured visitors. 'Up here, if you wrestle with a freshie they call you a poofter.'

Originally there had been some concern that Linda Kozlowski, being a New York girl, might have problems coping with the outback. They needn't have worried. Not only did she cope, she refused to use fakes when called on to bite into bush yams, a vegetable to be used only when no old boots were available for boiling. Said Hogan in praise: 'She's been thrown in swamps. She's been eaten alive by everything that crawls. She's had the skin scratched off her legs. Aussie crews aren't known for their patience and charm but she's sailed through. She hasn't complained once. We've made her an honorary Aussie.'

Anyone watching Hogan dressed in his snakeskin vest, his stockman's hat with crocodile teeth around the hatband – the teeth had to be imported from Asia – the machete-sized knife at his waist, could see he was playing Paul Hogan. He is always Paul Hogan, just as Clint Eastwood is always Clint, Burt Reynolds is always Burt and Ronald Reagan, whether in movies or the Oval Office, is always Ronald. Hogan admitted it was so. 'I've invented a character who looks like me, talks like me and has the same sense of humour as me. I didn't make a film about a hunch-backed German

Mick Dundee, like Hogan, is always himself, even at a smart New York gathering where anyone from out of town might feel uncomfortable.

U-boat commander because I'd have difficulty playing the part. I made a film about a Northern Territorian who acts a lot like me. I could probably play him in my sleep.'

If he was influenced by anyone, it was John Wayne, whom he saw at matinées long, long ago in the Granville Cinema. Hogan told *Fame* magazine: 'I subscribe to the John Wayne theory of acting. Always be yourself. If people like you they'll come to see you. Few remember the names of the characters Wayne played. All people knew was that they were going to see a John Wayne picture and they were probably in for a good time . . .'

And so the shooting went on in the wilderness, but even there Hogan wasn't safe from his admirers. In Sydney he can no longer go to the cricket because he would become the attraction instead of whoever was on the field. He accepts it as fame's penalty, but it niggles him. Nor can he take the kids up the street, or to an amusement park or to the zoo. But out there in Kakadu, among the dingoes and crocodiles and mosquitoes that zoom in like Spitfires, only noisier, where the sky stretches forever and falling stars leave a vivid scratch across night's deep blackness, he thought there'd be no problems. That was, until the day on location he was talking to Phil Jarratt, for an Australian *Playboy* magazine interview.

I've been here a few times and the characters I've met have been pretty extreme – dynamite fishermen, croc poachers and the like. They seek me out, these blokes. I might go to Darwin or Pine Creek or Katherine or wherever, I walk in the bar and the town murderer'll be over to say hello. Most of the time it's bloody good, you know? They're colourful characters; not mental giants some of them, mind you.

'It's not the usual fan/star relationship, is it?' Jarratt asked. 'They seem to regard you more as a mate.'

Hogan nodded.

Yeah, they seem to identify with me. A lot of people – blokes especially – come up and ask me for an autograph and you just know that they would never have asked anyone for an autograph in their lives. You get the odd bloke who looks like he's been bitin' the heads off bulls all morning, and he'll come over and say, ' 'Scuse me, Hoges, can I have your . . .'

NO
COMMERCIAL
TRAFFIC

DEPT OF   TRAFFIC

D ZONE

NO
NO STANDING
NO STOPPING
NO KIDDIN

DON'T
HONK

USALEN
E DESTROYED

When Mick Dundee loses his bearings in midtown Manhattan, he climbs a lamp-post (opposite) to see what's what. Then a friendly mounted policeman (above) takes him back to his hotel in style.

At that moment, to the astonishment of both, an elderly couple in matching safari suits stumbled out of the undergrowth, like they'd been picked by Central Casting for the rôle. Seeing Hogan, the husband yelled: 'G'day, Hoges, how're yer going?'

The woman turned in her tracks, not believing her eyes. 'It's not 'im!' she shrieked. 'Oh, it is, too! How're yer goin', Hoges?'

Hogan and Jarratt were silent for a moment, then Hogan asked: 'Did you organize that?'

Jarratt shook his head. 'Are you sure *you* didn't?'

Hogan laughed. 'Bloody amazing, isn't it?'

Production moved to New York. On paper it sounds simple, but for the cast and crew, who had spent weeks in the outback socializing with crocodiles and gum trees, the change was traumatic. Here people were shoulder to shoulder where before there had been only themselves (and the occasional tourist). They knew how 'Crocodile' Dundee felt. New Yorkers didn't have time to say 'G'day' to each other, let alone to strangers from the Antipodes. New Yorkers avoided eye contact because they could never be sure what was brewing behind the approaching eyes. But New Yorkers knew about business and if a film company, no matter where from, wanted to spend money making a movie, well, that was fine with New York: how can we help? Hogan found that New York authorities were much keener to assist than some of their counterparts in Australia, who believed film-making was an indulgence and that those involved should get a proper job.

In some ways the Australian attitude to film-making hasn't changed since the time, in 1976, when Dennis Weaver came to Sydney to make the 'Night of the Shark' episode of the *McCloud* television series. Weaver wanted to gallop across the Sydney Harbour Bridge, on which, incidentally, Hogan was no longer working by then, a spectacular stunt that would give the city excellent exposure on American television. The authorities shook their heads. But the Police Commissioner happened to be a fan of *McCloud* and suggested an illegal way. A car was stopped on one of the bridge's traffic lanes under the pretence that it was broken down. Weaver poked his head under the bonnet while the horses were brought in close to be mounted and the crew stood by ready to film. Weaver was poking away at the motor when a Department of Main Roads official, a guardian of the bridge with all the tact of a Kremlin commissar, arrived in an angry mood. 'What's going on here?' he demanded.

Weaver looked up, hoping that when he was recognized the official would relent. But not this one. 'This is going to be reported,' he said sternly.

Once the official had shuffled off, grumbling, to make his report, Weaver signalled the

Mick and Sue Charlton in one of the Big Apple scenes from *'Crocodile' Dundee*. Mick may be a fish out of water, but he's never over-awed.

director and shouted: 'Let's get what we can.' And away they went. They galloped across the bridge half a dozen times, disrupting traffic for an hour-and-a-half while crew members diverted officials, told lies, told jokes, even tap-danced, anything to keep the filming from being interrupted. They captured the scene but for the next three or four years a horse would only have to appear on a Sydney street to attract a horde of officials bearing books of rules and regulations and traffic citations.

In New York they would have permitted the Charge of the Light Brigade. 'They can't do enough for you in New York,' Hogan said.

You want police for the day, you tell them how many. You want the Statue of Liberty for a shot, they'll give it to you. You want Fifth Avenue, they'll close it for the day. They love film-makers and the city goes out of its way to co-operate. It's big business for them. And New Yorkers just accept it. They see a film crew on the street and it's like a bunch of blokes workin' on a hole in the road to them.

And again he revelled in the advantages of working for the cinema compared with television: 'We're filming in Fifth Avenue and Times Square and the police hold back all the traffic. In television you have to go into a little back street in Melbourne and pretend it's New York.' At times the lost souls of New York, the junkies, winos and lunatics, would see them filming and as a diversion to an endless day would wander on to the set. 'But,' said Hogan, 'you take no more notice of them than you do of buffaloes and crocodiles wanderin' around when you're in the Territory. It's the same sort of thing – a menacing environment.'

The style of New Yorkers, their cool approach to life, amused Hogan. Because of the tourism commercials, his face was not exactly unknown, but New Yorkers went out of their way to display their familiarity with famous faces, which are a dime a dozen in that city. If Jesus chose the Big Apple for the Second Coming he would be ignored until he was about to leave – and then presented with a bill. Hogan would go into a shop for shirts, impossible back home because half of Sydney would be in attendance offering sartorial advice. Without a hint of recognition, the salesman would say: 'Just through there, Mr

Dundee gets to know some of the locals in a New York bar. His artless amiability disarms everyone he meets.

Hogan.' The same in restaurants. The waiters would serve him without blinking, then when Hogan got up to leave would say: 'Hope you enjoyed your meal, Mr Hogan. G'day and goodnight.' It was a long way from Australia, where the waiter was likely to draw up a chair and chat. Hogan reckoned you could walk down a New York street naked with your head on fire and no one would take any notice. They'd seen it all before.

New Yorkers were blasé about life, but when they stopped bustling and hustling Hogan found them friendly. In movies this is not generally shown. In movies New Yorkers are seen as threatening. Those not about to mug you will steal a parking space from under your car's nose. Hogan saw them differently, as affable people happy to share a drink or, as the movie showed, a line or two of illegal substances.

There was one mugging in 'Crocodile' Dundee, portrayed in a way that had American audiences cheering in their seats. Dundee is confronted with a mugger with a small knife. 'You call *that* a knife,' says Dundee with a smile, then produces a blade that could lay waste the forests of the Amazon. '*This* is a knife.' The mugger flees, and one suspects that next day he went to the employment office seeking a career change.

Hogan was well aware that the agreeableness of New Yorkers was a good selling point. 'Some people said the mayor should give me a plaque because I show New Yorkers can be friendly,' he said. 'The mounted policeman brings me back to the hotel on his horse when I get lost on Fifth Avenue. And I show that

'*This* is a knife': the famous mugging scene in *Crocodile* brought roars of approval from audiences everywhere.

subways can be romantic places – the crowd helps the girl to get together with me.' Also he understood that New Yorkers don't mind laughing at themselves and the rest of America doesn't mind laughing at New York. It was an each-way bet that worked.

The small budget meant long days, up to fifteen hours in locations ranging from Times Square to a punk barber shop in SoHo. The only interruption to their schedule was a day off when Hurricane Gloria came close. 'We get one of them every day at home,' joked Hogan (or was it Dundee?). 'We call it a sea breeze.'

As the shooting progressed, Hogan, Cornell and Faiman began to get a good feeling about the movie. People were interested. Extras laughed in the right places. For one scene 300 extras were needed in a New York subway station so that Mick Dundee could walk over their shoulders to reach his girlfriend, as sheep dogs scramble over the backs of sheep to control the mob. 'Everywhere they're supposed to laugh, they laugh,' Hogan said. 'Humour is different all over the world, but this movie would be funny in Japan.' And then, with the cockiness that's been a part of him all his life, he said confidently to a New York reporter: 'I wanted to make an Australian movie that's entertaining all over the world, because if we don't start making movies with wide entertainment appeal our movie industry will die. And this one's a money-maker – it's not made to win awards at the Ethiopian film festival.'

In other words, long before '*Crocodile*' *Dundee* was in the can, as they say in the industry, Hogan was confident that not only would it do good business at the Australian box office, it would perform well on the international circuit.

'Blessed are the deal-makers, for they shall inherit the industry.'
Anon.

John Cornell sat near the swimming pool in the gardens of the Bel Air Hotel, breathing the thick air of Los Angeles and waiting for the telephone to ring. Waiters hurried past bearing trays of cool drinks. Some of the old names of Hollywood strolled past in search of their yesterdays. Tony Curtis ambled past in search of his tomorrows. Producers, lawyers and studio bosses were scattered around doing deals, or in some cases pretending to, for this was pure Hollywood, where the fantasy doesn't stop at the studio gates. Sitting near Cornell was Terry Jackman, the marketing specialist contracted to help sell *'Crocodile' Dundee* to the American market. Both men were relaxed. They knew the telephone would soon start ringing. And it did. It didn't stop ringing for days.

Cornell was well pleased with the movie's release in Australia, as he should have been, because within days it had set new box-office records and looked likely to break all records for ticket sales. In its first week in 70 cinemas it took $2 million. In the second week the takings went to $2.4 million, then to $2.6 million the third week. With few exceptions, the critics had heaped praise on the movie. The one sour note came from Phillip Adams,

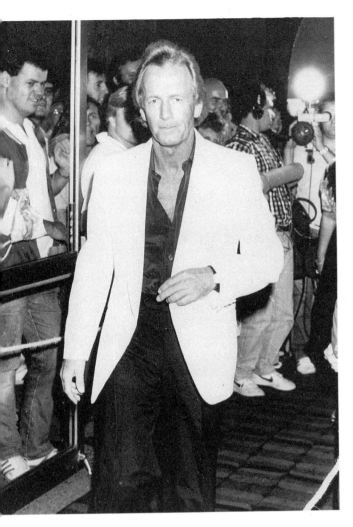

Hogan arrives for the Australian première of *'Crocodile' Dundee*, a film which surely pointed the way forward for the Australian film industry.

could never get Hogan to talk intellectually about his comedy, to come up with some sort of philosophical stance, as had Spike Milligan, Barry Humphries and Woody Allen. The only stance Hogan took was that being a comedian was a funny way to make a living but if he could make people laugh it was a job well done. Adams' attack may also have had something to do with Hogan's frequently stated contempt for what he called the 'wankers' of the Australian movie industry, the producers, directors, actors and writers that Adams had loudly supported over the years. Hogan had held nothing back when he talked to John Baxter for *Cinema Papers*:

There are people making boring little films that are about nothing, and then, because the public doesn't like them, they wank off about how it's too clever for 'em or it's going over their heads. You kid yourself that you can go off with your little film under your arm and walk into any of the international theatre chains and say, 'It's an Australian movie!' and they're going to go, 'Oh, wow! Let's have a look at it!' They're more inclined just to shrug. Unless they've got a little art cinema chain in Los Angeles, you're going to end up on Home Box Office.

He told another reporter that the 'wankers' who produced films using public money made it hard for others who came along: 'You'll never make the *Out of Africa/Passage to India/Ghandi*-type movies in this country unless you make commercial successes so that the big investors and the big distributors are going to have the faith to put the money up.'

While acknowledging *Breaker Morant* as a good movie, he said its problem was a lack of money. 'It's a good story, but when the enemy charges over the hill there's fifteen of 'em. Theatre owners won't put that on the big screen, regardless of the merit and the value that's in it.' He believed the sort of movies Australia could make would be similar to *Arthur*, *Back to the Future*, *Every Which Way But Loose* and *Romancing the Stone* – 'what I call proper movies'.

Because of his position as chairman of the Australian Film Commission, Adams' comments were widely publicized. But in the

advertising man, radio personality, commentator, newspaper columnist, chairman of the Australian Film Commission and champagne socialist, who thought the film was listless and Hogan's performance lacklustre:

The film fails (although I've no doubt it will be a great financial success) because of its confusion of purpose. While packaged to look like *Indiana Jones*, it doesn't deliver as an adventure story, a few lunging crocs notwithstanding. We expect it to be a riotous comedy, yet it's nothing like as funny as it ought to be, particularly on the verbal level . . .

The attack, spread over a page of *The Australian*, was delivered for several reasons, all peculiar to Adams. One may have been that he

Hogan camp they weren't saying much. Cornell dismissed Adams by saying that he and Hogan never replied to critics, because 'a boxer never jumps from the ring to hit the big-mouth at the ringside who keeps telling him he's a bum'.

There was a minor kerfuffle in the Australian film industry when Cornell and Hogan refused to enter *'Crocodile' Dundee* in the Australian Film Institute's annual awards, basically because too often awards were given to movies that ran two nights in a back-street cinema. The Federal Arts Minister, Barry Cohen, joined in by saying the Australian Film Institute was against commercialization. 'I guess *'Crocodile' Dundee* wasn't entered because the producers didn't need to be insulted by people who will vote for a movie no one wants to see,' Cohen said. The film institute got over the embarrassment by giving *'Crocodile' Dundee* an award anyway – one for special achievement.

What Hogan said about Australian movies contained much truth. The Australian film industry has led a turbulent life. Some of the first movies made anywhere came out of Australia. The country's first feature film, *The Story of the Kelly Gang*, was produced in 1906, only three years after the first significant American movie, *The Great Train Robbery*. The industry flourished until the 1920s, when it was swamped by American imports. In the 1970s it was resuscitated when the Australian Film Commission was established, the period producing *Picnic at Hanging Rock*, *Sunday Too Far Away*, *The Getting of Wisdom*, *My Brilliant Career*, *The Chant of Jimmie Blacksmith* and *Breaker Morant*. They were, for the most part, fine films that gave the Australian industry an excellent image overseas. But it was an image confined to the art houses; the movies were not released in 1,000 cinemas across the United States. The *Mad Max* movies, which could have been shot anywhere in the world, were the first with truly international appeal. In the 1980s numerous films were made that were so awful they were banned from the Golden Turkey Awards on the grounds that they provided unfair competition. Many were never released and ended up gathering dust on the shelves of undiscerning video stores. Often

made by shonky producers who discovered money under various beds, they sometimes left a trail of unpaid bills and actors and crew begging for their wages. These were made solely to obtain generous benefits under the tax concession scheme. The Australian film industry was haemorrhaging badly until *'Crocodile' Dundee* came to the rescue and, in spite of what Phillip Adams may have thought, pointed the way to the only possible future.

The way *'Crocodile' Dundee* was designed to appeal to international audiences who had never been inside an art cinema was criticized by two Melbourne academics with, one suspects, time on their hands. Jo Crawford and Ruth Abbey, of Monash University's Department of Politics, complained that the movie distorted the Australian way of life and was popular with American audiences because it said nothing that could be seen as a threat to America's preconceived ideas. To back up their argument they cited the outback dinner at which Dundee offered to barbecue a goanna – the meat on the tail is, incidentally, delicious – for Sue, the American journalist. Dundee, of course, stayed with a can of beans. Another example from the academics was a scene showing Dundee shaving. When Sue watched he used a large knife, but when she wasn't looking he used an ordinary razor. Crawford and Abbey claimed that Dundee's apparent 'distance from civilization is further reduced when, appearing to tell the time naturally from the position of the sun, we see him cast a discreet glance in the direction of the nearest wristwatch'. The academics added: 'If we desire to protect local mores, idioms, symbols and values, then these must be reflected in our cultural product . . . It would seem we are faced with the classical Faustian dilemma, the choice of selling our soul or becoming impoverished martyrs to the cause of cultural fidelity.' Hogan wouldn't have put it in those words, but he had been saying much the same for years. Export or perish! And for export the movies had to appeal to the world, not merely a bunch of academics and 'wankers'.

Long before Cornell was installed in the Bel Air Hotel, the big American distributors had known of *'Crocodile' Dundee*. Each has a network of scouts searching the world for independently-made movies likely to appeal to American audiences. In fact Henry Seggerman, Paramount Pictures' vice-president of acquisitions, whose job was to keep track of the world's independent film-makers, had contacted Cornell before 'Crocodile' Dundee had gone into production. 'How are we going to make a deal to buy your film?' he asked Cornell.

Cornell had his own plans. Even though he had been pressured by investors to secure their returns by pre-selling the movie to Hollywood, Cornell was convinced that the only way was to arrive in Los Angeles bearing the completed product. He did his research by organizing two showings in California and was gratified when the audiences laughed at the right times, enjoyed the outback scenery and, above all, loved the hero. So when the telephone began ringing at the Bel Air Hotel, Cornell was in a position of strength. One of the first he talked to was Twentieth Century-Fox, under the umbrella of Australian-born media mogul Rupert Murdoch. They turned it down, a costly blunder, but did nicely by picking up the world rights. But almost from the start Cornell had leaned towards Paramount, liking the way its executives operated.

'There's a lot of bullshit in this town,' said Cornell. 'Everyone you meet is a movie producer. That's why I always introduce myself as a tractor salesman. But there's a lot less of it at Paramount. They tell you what they think rather than what they think you want to hear.'

After ten days of negotiations, a deal was signed with Paramount. The company paid about £3.5 million for the North American rights, but agreed to pay more than the usual royalties from the film's theatrical release and subsequent airing on video and cable television. Paramount immediately announced it would spend more than the movie's budget on promotion because, as Sid Ganis, the studio's marketing president, explained, the movie did not have a frame of reference familiar to Americans and Canadians. 'We have to get out there and let them know what it is about.'

The movie's fish-out-of-water theme was familiar to Paramount, which almost had a copyright on the genre, having produced such lucrative examples as *Trading Places*, *48 Hours* and *Beverly Hills Cop*. But some adjustments were needed before the movie was ready for the American market. Quotation marks were placed around 'Crocodile' in case people thought it was a swamp movie. It should be understood that everything in Hollywood is categorized and a movie is never just a movie. The advertising was planned, the poster showing Dundee parting the skyscrapers of Manhattan with the teaser: 'He's survived the most hostile and primitive land known to man. Now all he's got to do is make it through a week in New York.' Seven minutes were cut from early sequences so that Dundee could get to New York seven minutes quicker, the Americans not being noted for their patience or for the length of their attention span. Or maybe they had in mind Alfred Hitchcock's advice that 'the length of a film should be directly related to the endurance of the human bladder'. Some expressions, like 'stone the bloody crows' and 'sticky beak', were removed because they were unknown to Americans.

After recovering from the attack of the eagle, Hogan went to the United States to embark on one of the biggest promotional campaigns ever undertaken by one person, criss-crossing America to increase his profile, giving some 300 interviews until hotels and airports and conference rooms were blurred into one; if this is 2.30 p.m. Tuesday it must be the *Washington Post*. It was a gruelling task and sometimes his tiredness showed with flashes of irritation, though Hogan generally managed to conceal his exasperation at being confronted with the same predictable set of questions. An interview on the Cable News Network was typical:

'The film has been praised by the critics in Australia,' suggested the interviewer.

'Yeah,' said Hogan, settling into a laconic vein. 'That surprised me because I didn't make it for them.'

'How have American audiences reacted?'

'They laughed in all the places I wanted them to, and in a couple of places I didn't know they would laugh at.'

'No trouble with your accent?'

'No, I speak English. They might have had trouble with one or two of the New York accents, but they managed mine all right.'

'Let's assume that *'Crocodile' Dundee* is a huge success. I suppose there'll be a *Return of 'Crocodile' Dundee*?'

'Oh maybe, I don't know. I've done a movie this year, now I'm on holidays.'

'That's the Australian attitude, isn't it? You look forward to the weekend?'

'Yup!'

Hogan was splashed in *Newsweek*, *People* and *US*. Every major newspaper devoted columns to him, dwelling especially on his transformation from Sydney Harbour Bridge rigger to television star via a talent contest in which he made fools of the judges. This fascinated Americans, because it reinforced their beloved myth that anyone can achieve success – that a man digging ditches can one day make it to the White House if he chooses. The *Chicago Tribune* wanted to know the difference between Australian and American humour. Hogan obliged:

I think the Poms and the Aussies share the same sort of humour and outlook. We love to poke fun at our leaders, and no one's sacred. By contrast, Americans tend to have a lot of sacred cows. I mean people will gladly criticize Reagan's foreign policy or whatever, but they'll never crack jokes about the size of Nancy's head. It's strange, 'cause there's a lot of great comedians in America, but hardly any tradition of political satire. I think Americans take their politicians – and politics – very seriously.

USA Today was interested in his opinion of Hollywood producers. Hogan had an answer:

Most of the people I've met haven't been stupid. They haven't come up with ridiculous propositions. Those Hollywood caricature producers – the big fat man with the cigar – they're not at the top of the industry, usually. They hang around in restaurants, get seen a lot, and talk in very loud voices in restaurants: 'Robert Redford, he's not getting the part.' They're sort of cartoon characters. When you get to the major studios, the people who are in charge of developing, they're usually brighter and more down to earth than you think. In other words, Hollywood is not full of jerks.

The Gannett News Service wanted to know about his success. Hogan was ready.

No level of success would surprise me now. The most radical step was the one from construction worker to TV star overnight. I wouldn't run for prime minister, though, because I'd probably get the job. I'd only do it if I could be a benevolent dictator. But in a democracy, no one person will ever make a difference.

He appeared on network television shows, including the *Johnny Carson Show*, on which he was censored for saying 'balls'.

When *'Crocodile' Dundee* opened in 879 American and Canadian theatres in the northern autumn, the faith Hogan and Cornell had in their product was justified. It took (US)$31 million in its first 17 days. By the end of the year it had taken an amazing (US)$117 million, making it the most successful film ever released in North America in autumn and the most successful foreign film. The previous record for an autumn release was held by Goldie Hawn's *Private Benjamin*. The best-performing foreign film had been the British-made *Chariots of Fire*, which took (US)$60 million. In the language of the trade publication *Variety*, *Crocodile* was 'wrestling fine' in New York, 'chewing loudly' in Los Angeles, 'grinning' in St Louis, 'nifty' in Kansas City, 'munching' in Chicago and 'heroic' in Washington.

At last Paramount relaxed and discreetly enquired whether a sequel was possible. 'The surprising thing is that the appeal of the movie defies demographics and geographics,' said the chairman of Paramount, Frank Mancuso. 'We're getting the infrequent moviegoers, people who go to the movies once or twice a year. Typically, 25 per cent of your prints, in the major cities, bring in 75 per cent of the revenue. But *Crocodile* is different because it has such strength in middle-sized cities.' The comments of Carl Kahn, owner of ten cinemas in New Mexico, were typical. 'The movie has cross-cultural appeal,' he said. 'Everyone's coming out for it – Indians, Hispanics and Anglos. *'Crocodile' Dundee* makes people feel good. It has an innocence.' The owner of eight cinemas in Colorado, Stan Pratt, agreed. 'It's nice there's room for a film that doesn't offend the masses.' Perhaps the syndicated film columnist for the *Chicago Tribune*, Gene Siskel, summed it up best when he said: 'The lesson here is that there is a massive audience that wants clean, wholesome entertainment. It may be a slightly older audience and they may not go to the movies often, but they will go when they hear from their friends that it's safe to go to the movies again.'

The film reviewers generally applauded the film. The *Philadelphia Inquirer* said: 'Hogan has combined a riotous and affectionate spoof of entrenched machismo Down Under with a disarmingly droll satire of the way urban Americans choose – or are forced – to live. 'Crocodile' Dundee goes down as enjoyably as Foster's, and it's easy to overlook the natural skill of Hogan's work. He has Harrison Ford's gift for arch asides on his own character and he's funnier.' Raved the Los Angeles *Herald Examiner*: 'He wins everyone over with wit and charm. It's so wonderful to have a hero who is not using knives and violence and whom you really liked.' The *New York Post* was a little more restrained: 'The undeveloped script is vulgar in a populist way; it has enough pleasant touches to hold things together. Hogan, who is slight of build, displays a definite charisma (more than, say, Chuck Norris) and he is the major reason for seeing this movie.' The *Los Angeles Times* thought the film was 'certainly no gem of originality, but it doesn't really have to be. Everything in the movie is designed to show off Hogan, and secondarily, Kozlowski, to their best advantage: to sell us on Kozlowski's bemused grin, sleek thighs and killer eyes, on Hogan's warm equanimity and icy competence.' The *New York Times* said 'Crocodile' Dundee embodied a legend, and it 'seems his larger-than-life character is as dear to the Australian self-image as Paul Bunyan or Davy Crockett are to our own . . . It's a romantic fantasy where logic isn't always of prime importance and a light comedy that follows its own internal laws with charm. But the most popular film ever to be shown in Australia? This perhaps tells us more about the Australian self-image than it does about the film's value.' The *Washington Post* said: 'Here's a welcome departure – a he-man who doesn't sweat steroids. 'Crocodile' Dundee is a human-sized, humble hero with better-than-average smarts and a nice smile. Where Rambo would grunt and fire off a nuclear arrow, Dundee would think a minute, then maybe lob a tin of beans.' Probably the most important review came from the respected Vincent Canby of the *New York Times*, who all but gushed:

'Crocodile' Dundee is a nice though scarcely side-splitting comedy. In place of gags of falling-down funniness, it has the genial, self-assured personality of its star, who comes on as an extension of the tanned, breezy, welcoming character featured in all those Australian Tourist Commission spots. Though I suspect Mr Hogan uses only about one-tenth of his comic capabilities in 'Crocodile' Dundee, he's evidently using the right one-tenth for the purposes of the movie. Like the tourism commercials, 'Crocodile' Dundee successfully creates the impression that there is something approaching a smogless, egalitarian American heaven on earth, though it's called Australia, where men are still men and women thank God for it . . . Though much of it takes place in New York, the film is possibly the most effectively indigenous Australian movie ever to come to this country. It expresses the infinite possibilities represented by those spectacular beaches and under-populated landscapes we see behind Mr Hogan in his television spots. For some years we've been importing vast numbers of automobiles that once would have been manufactured in Detroit. It's possible that, in 'Crocodile' Dundee, we're now importing an ideal we used to think was exclusively American.

What Canby said was echoed by several commentators. In fact, pop sociologists had a field day with 'Crocodile' Dundee, dissecting it, holding it up to the light, probing and pulling, as they searched for meanings that weren't there. Or if they were there they hadn't been deliberately included by Hogan. He had repeatedly said that in 'Crocodile' Dundee he had done no more than produce a movie he hoped would make people feel good. Why they felt good was not his concern. But it kept the pop sociologists occupied and they were at liberty to dissect it any way they wished after they'd paid for their cinema ticket. Bums on seats were Hogan's concern . . . and mums on seats as well, because the film had been designed for family consumption. Some sections of the media had suggested it was hopelessly out of sync with such sexually explicit movies as *Blue Velvet*.

Pride of place in Mick Dundee's wardrobe was held by the snakeskin jacket, no doubt made from a recent conquest.

'I haven't seen it,' said Hogan, 'but *Blue Velvet* has probably been good for us. After you come out, from what I hear, you need to have your soul cleansed. And for that, my simple little comedy's just the thing.'

Not only was it clean but it had hit an American nerve, and that nerve jolted memories of the hazy, golden days of the past, the Normal Rockwell days when the worst your kids could do was steal apples from an orchard and violence was what you saw in a James Cagney movie. As some commentators had suggested, those days might not have existed. But they were there, deep within the minds and souls of Middle America. The American playwright Neil Simon, author of *Barefoot in the Park*, *The Odd Couple*, *Brighton Beach Memoirs* and *Biloxi Blues*, suggested that *'Crocodile' Dundee* was an American success because the cultures of the two countries were similar.

They are countries which are almost as old as each other. There isn't a history that goes way, way back. We seem to have the same attitudes, which I think is why it's working in reverse. It seems that *'Crocodile' Dundee* is probably America the way it was some years back, but it's very refreshing to see it again, to see a swaggering character.

Even commentators in Australia, looking at its phenomenal American success, attempted to analyse it from half a world away. Frank Campbell, senior lecturer in Australian studies at Deakin University, Victoria, argued that Dundee was a 'soft *Rambo*, calling gently to the frightened, isolated American within, calling him out to conquer his fears and return to the verities of the golden age. Paul Hogan has gazed deep into America. Whether America ever was an open-hearted land of trust matters not in the reality of endemic fear and distrust – for two brief hours of cinematic darkness there is joy.' And all Hogan thought he was doing was making a nice little movie.

When the movie opened in the United States, Hogan did not throw an extravagant party in the accepted Hollywood style. He was not seen with a crowd of well-wishers in one of the expensive Los Angeles restaurants near Rodeo Drive, his hand being shaken, his back slapped and his ego massaged as the hordes told him what an excellent fellow he was – and

can we do a deal? He was sick of people trying to do deals. Everywhere he went in Hollywood he was faced with deals. He had only to walk into a reception and in moments it was like a deal-makers' convention. Instead, with Faiman, Cornell and Kozlowski, he hired a limousine and went around Los Angeles looking with enormous pleasure at the queues forming outside cinemas. They entered some and stood at the back, revelling in the laughter and applause, then called at a friend's place for a few beers.

'How do you feel?' Cornell asked.

'You'd have to smack me across the face to wipe the smile off,' said Hogan. 'I thought the movie would work but I never expected this.'

The movie's success meant there was not a lot of time to enjoy the pleasures on offer at the Bel Air Hotel, including the swimming pool. Film scripts showered on him like confetti on a bride, although most of the rôles offered had little in common with his personality. He was nominated – and won – the Hollywood Foreign Press Association's Golden Globe Award for best actor. *W* magazine put him on top of the 'in' list for 1987. *People* magazine listed him as one of the 25 most interesting people of 1986, calling him 'a wry, laconic sex symbol – a Sam Shepherd with humour'. *Life* magazine named him as one of the year's top guns along with such stars as Tom Cruise and Sigourney Weaver. *Newsday* insisted that he was going to buy a house in Los Angeles and take up permanent residence – news to Hogan, who couldn't see himself living anywhere but Sydney. He made the *Man Watcher*'s annual list of the world's most watchable men, the selections based on appearance, charisma, carriage, posture, grooming and ability to communicate, provoking chuckles from his mates on the Harbour Bridge. It got to the stage where he could not appear in public without being mobbed.

'Hey, croc man,' someone would yell from across the street. Hogan would shudder, hoping he could walk away, but there would be nowhere to walk because another person would confront him with a line from the movie, or a middle-aged woman would sidle up and say huskily: 'You can put a shrimp on my barbie any time.' He realized the truth of

Charles Laughton's rueful comment of an earlier decade: 'Every time I walk into a restaurant I get not only soup but an impersonation of Captain Bligh.'

Peter Faiman was also in demand. Suddenly he found himself besieged with offers on anything from television sit-coms to feature movies. He was hot. And when you're hot in Hollywood you need either a fire tender or a place to breathe. Faiman decided on fresh air and, taking the advice dispensed by Hogan in his tourism commercials, perused the airline timetables for Australia. A quietly spoken man vastly experienced in television but with only one movie to his credit, albeit a blockbuster, Faiman was bemused by the offers. 'It's very flattering but it's overwhelming, being an instant star in this town of instant stars,' he said. 'I haven't been off the phone and I have been "doing lunch", "talking meetings" and "doing afternoon teas", talking about movies, specials, sit-coms, business deals, management, you name it. At this stage I want to get home and sift it all and put everything into perspective before I make any decisions. We knew we had something but none of us in our wildest dreams expected it to be the smash hit it has become.'

While Hogan and Cornell were, not surprisingly, gratified by the adulation in the United States and at times a little bewildered by its intensity, they couldn't hang around. There was more work to be done on 'Crocodile' Dundee, which opened in Britain for the 1986 Christmas season. It got away to a good start when the British critics generally approved of what they saw, though they regarded it as not an ambitious film. The Guardian commented: 'The man clearly knows what he is doing, building up a ludicrous image and then upending it with wry charm.' The Independent agreed:

Hogan's persona is the film's small secret. He is shrewd without being worldly, naive without being at all vulnerable. He encourages the other characters and the audience to under-estimate him, and then when he proves them wrong reaps a disproportionate harvest of esteem. Pretending to be a primitive so as to survive by a mild sophistication seems to be the Australian national sport.

Bernard Levin, The Times' gnome-like intellectual, went over the top. Or maybe it was a joke for members of Mensa.

'Crocodile' Dundee is the perfectly pure, wholly innocent (innocent in both senses of the word) figure who is found in the epic literature of all the nations which have such sagas. He is Beowulf and King Arthur, Roland and Oliver, Candide and Bertie Wooster, Prince Charming and Bilbo Baggins and Robin Hood. He is even – indeed, above all – Wagner's Parsifal, 'durch Mitleid wissend, der reine Tor' (the pure fool, made wise by pity) . . .

Eh? And who in hell was Bilbo Baggins?

Elsewhere the media got down to the old nitty-gritty of sex, or more precisely down to their belief that Hogan was a sex symbol, a tag he found faintly ridiculous, more so when he opened fan mail from 14-year-old girls.

'It's very embarrassing,' he said. 'They would probably get on well with my youngest son, who is twelve.'

He also had a word to say in support of the royal family, which had on occasions been the butt of Hogan's humour: 'I have a lot of time for the royal family. The way the press goes after them is disgusting. They're the biggest asset the Poms have – they should restore them to their rightful place. The royals are vital for tourism. People don't come to Britain to loll around on the beaches.'

The movie opened in Britain with the cash registers jangling as loudly as they had in the United States. So many fans crowded the Leicester Square Odeon Theatre that staff had to use loud hailers to control them. In its first week Crocodile broke the West End box-office record by taking $365,982. Soon the movie was screening throughout Europe, in West Germany as Krokodil Dundee and Italy as Croccodillo.

But there was still Japan to conquer, the biggest movie market outside the United States. Before he left Sydney for Tokyo in February, 1987, Hogan explained the importance of the various markets.

Whatever you earn from a movie, 70 per cent of it comes out of America. Right now, we've broken box-office records in every country we've gone into, including places like Switzerland and Holland and Brazil. But in Brazil people pay about 80 cents to go to the movies. In Japan they pay about $35, so you're better off having a moderate success in Japan than a blockbuster in Brazil.

That may be so, but Western humour, the slick throwaway line, the witty repartee, does not always translate comfortably into Japanese. And maybe Hogan was tired from his British and American promotional campaigns and found difficulty turning on the charm. It couldn't always be tapped like a keg of Foster's. The crowded media conference at the Imperial Hotel could not quite figure out this inscrutable Australian.

'What is your opinion of Japanese food?' he was asked.

'I had some vegetables last night that I think had been dipped in chloroform.'

When the translation sank in there was silence. The best way to insult Japanese hospitality is by criticizing the food. Aware of his gaffe, Hogan hurriedly added: 'No insult meant.'

His gags failed to work. At one stage he asked his interpreter if the joke had been successfully translated. Another time, when he made a serious point that comedy was best when it offended nobody, the media laughed. A critic in the magazine *City Roads* summed it up when he said, 'It may be there are many of the gags in the movie which I did not understand.'

To a photographer who wanted to picture him outside the hotel holding a stuffed crocodile, he snapped: 'I do this 700 times a day.' Nor did he help the Australian tourist trade when in his usual exaggerated style he said: 'There are more Japanese tourists going to Australia already than we have accommodation for. There's not enough room on the planes.' Actually it wasn't that much of an exaggeration. So popular had Australia become for tourists that Sydney, at least, had a shortage of hotel rooms. But it wasn't what the Australian Tourist Commission wanted the Japanese to hear. Still, he was politely received. A *Motion Picture Times* journalist tried to get into the Australian mood by incorporating into her article the salutation 'G'day, mate.' Unfortunately she rendered it in Japanese script as the plural 'G'day, mates' and used it to sign off instead of greet. Another writer in the same journal had the last say: 'It's surprising that Australians are able to make such a movie. Just until a few years ago they were unpolished yokels.'

Ouch! But Hogan had other concerns on the horizon and one was the 1987 Academy Awards.

'Hollywood's all right. It's the pictures that are bad.'
Orson Welles

The producers of the 59th annual Academy Awards were a trifle nervous. The opening was less than two weeks away and they hadn't heard from Paul Hogan, who was to deliver the first speech of the night or, more accurately, the first jokes. Speeches were for politicians. Hollywood wanted humour – something to ease the inner fears the psychiatrists may have missed. But, dammit, they couldn't get Hogan to indicate what he would say. Good grief, the fellow was Australian and he might drop his trousers . . . or worse, say something rude about Hollywood.

Hogan, still in Australia, was unperturbed. He had a few ideas running loose in his head. He knew, for instance, that he could not tell crocodile jokes, because they were eating people in Australia and no matter which way you looked at it, there was not a lot to tickle the funnybone in people being chewed. So no crocodile jokes. And too much Australian slang would be a non-starter because Americans had not long since come to terms with 'G'day' and 'sheila' and might not relate to, say, 'May your chooks turn to emus and kick your dunny down.' That was out. After thinking about it for a few days, Hogan decided he would drop a few lines similar to some he had

delivered to an Australian Logie Award night a few years back. He would provide 'the opinion of somebody who was a television viewer rather than a member of the Hollywood scene. Sort of like someone who has seen them on television for years and thought they were too long and that there was some awful speeches and back-slapping, and those sort of embarrassin' things.'

Then the producers wanted to know what he would wear. 'What about the hat?' they asked, referring to Mick Dundee's headgear.

'Nah, I don't think so.'

'The gear, then. Can you wear the gear?'

'I'll wear a dinner-suit. I don't brush up too bad in a dinner-suit, y'know.'

Even three days before the big event Hogan wasn't sure what he would say. With his wife Noelene he arrived in Hollywood, perhaps the calmest person in a neurotic town once described as a place 'where inferior people have a way of making superior people feel inferior'. He sketched out his lines, gave them to the Oscar producers for the autocue, climbed into a dinner-suit then into a stretch limousine and set off. He was warmly received by the big crowd outside the auditorium, several of whom wanted to see his *Dundee* knife. He didn't take it to the Academy Awards; it would have spoiled the cut of his suit.

Then, before such celebrities as Elizabeth Taylor, Bob Hope, Oliver Stone, Jane Fonda and Bette Davis, and 300 million viewers around the world, including half of Australia, he marched to the podium and, with a small grin, said: 'G'day, viewers. This is my first time at the Academy Awards. I've usually watched it on television and for that reason I've been asked to come out here and speak to my peers on behalf of the television audience . . . G'day, peers.'

Laughter rippled through the audience.

This of course is the big event of show business and the atmosphere here is pure electricity. But as a television show it does tend to go slightly off the boil, particularly as you drift into the third and fourth hour. Now what can we do about it? Firstly,

After a super-whammo like *'Crocodile' Dundee*, where can you go next? Hogan gave himself a hard act to follow.

hah, winners, when you make your speech, it's a good tip to remember the three Gs – be gracious, be grateful and get off. Secondly, don't be too humble tonight because we have up here a second envelope. Don't get up to the stage and say, 'I don't deserve this award.' If you really feel you don't deserve an Academy Award, just give us a wave from your seat and we'll open the second envelope and give it to someone else . . .

They liked that one. Hogan had by now visibly relaxed as he remembered that the size of the audience did not matter. An entertainer can bomb just as disastrously before 50 people as before 300 million. But Hogan wasn't bombing. The audience was even laughing in the right places. 'If you don't have a speech prepared, come and see me backstage in the next ten or fifteen minutes . . . I've got a heap of spares. They cover every category.' He looked at the envelope in his hand.

This one here's for the outstanding taxidermist. They're brief, they're sincere. I'll give you a little sample. 'I'd like to thank my Momma, my Poppa, the good Lord above . . .' oh, no, that's the country music awards. Most importantly tonight, most nominees will be on camera when they announce the winner. Please, nominees, let's not have the spectacle of all non-winners givin' us this one.

Hogan looked directly at the camera with a sickly smile out of vaudeville.

This is the old so-glad-he-won-instead-of-me smile. Think of the television audience, give us a bit of variety. Y'know, maybe one or two of you could burst into tears. Stormin' out of the building in a huff would be nice. What's wrong with a bit of good old-fashioned booing . . .

His speech was bubbling along nicely. Occasionally he tugged an earlobe, a habit he shared with Johnny Carson. All traces of nervousness had gone, yet if anyone had a reason for the jitters that night it was Hogan. Not since the days of Errol Flynn and Peter Finch had an Australian actor been so much in the Hollywood limelight. Also, *'Crocodile' Dundee* had been nominated for the Best Original Screenplay award, though Hogan had long since dismissed his chances. Before leaving Australia, he said he hadn't a hope of winning because awards were more often given to

No qualms for Hogan about that first moment of on-screen osculation – and Linda Kozlowski seems quite happy about it too.

serious movies than box-office successes. 'Give me a choice between picking up eleven awards and grossin' 400 million dollars and I think I'd lean towards the gross,' he had said. He was right. The award went to Woody Allen for *Hannah and Her Sisters* and the gross for *'Crocodile' Dundee* was heading towards $400 million.

He used his Oscar nomination for his next lines.

I'm nominated tonight and I realize I'm not exactly the odds-on favourite, but I travelled 13,000 miles to be here for this. I come from the other side of the planet. And if they read out someone's else name instead of mine, it's not going to be pretty. I'll probably spill blood. But anyway, listen, most important, the producer of this programme, Sam Goldwyn, said everyone's really tense out there. Go out and see if you can get them to relax.

He looked sharply at the camera, paused briefly, then asked:

Why? You didn't come here to relax. If you want to relax, stay at home and watch it on television. That'll relax yer. No, fellow workers, brothers, workmates, you're here to sweat. This programme is live. There's about 1,000 million people watchin' you. So you remember, one wrong word, one foolish gesture and your whole career could go down in flames. Hold that thought and have a nice night, d'yer hear?

Then it was over. For four minutes he had been in front of the biggest audience of his life, for 240 seconds he had kept amused a crowd of vastly experienced performers, seemingly with the casualness of a bloke spinning a yarn at the pub. And that had been the secret of his success since leaving the Harbour Bridge. He had never really changed. There was no need for change because the formula, if such it could be called, had international appeal. Australia felt a little proud that night.

There was another award for Hogan that week. Three nights after the Oscars, he was to be presented with a Logie award in Melbourne in recognition of his contribution to television. Because he would be 30,000 feet over the Pacific at the time, the presentation was made by an Australian television reporter in Los Angeles.

The reporter and crew duly arrived and chatted to Hogan, who said, with mild sarcasm: 'Now you want me to make a Logie speech?'

'Yes, we'd like that,' said the reporter, gritting his teeth and hoping Hogan wasn't in a playful mood.

He was. He looked at the camera, and in a voice like a schoolboy chanting his lesson in class, said: 'Oh, gosh, what . . . a . . . surprise . . . and . . . a . . . thrill.' Then he reverted to his normal drawl, for he had a small point to make and that was that it had been many a moon since he had contributed anything at all to television.

Thank you to whoever gave me this. I think, thank you, I'm not sure. These are handed out for services to television. And I haven't made any television since 1983. A more thin-skinned person than myself might assume that you're sayin' the best service I can perform for Australian television is not to make any. But I'm not thin-skinned. A more thin-skinned person than myself might also think it was an extraordinary coincidence that you chose to give me this award when you knew I was out of the country and therefore didn't have to invite me to the party. But I'm not thin-skinned, so I'll accept this award and try to look on the bright side, which is that I won't have to sit there tonight while someone makes an attempt on the world's longest, most boring Logie acceptance speech . . .

Unshaven and weary, Hogan landed at Sydney Airport on Saturday morning. He was met by a newspaper reporter who had not unreasonably expected Hogan to be at least a little excited over his Academy Awards appearance. Hogan was the opposite, holding true to his earlier statements that award ceremonies did not mean much and life could get along smoothly without them.

'I never take any award seriously,' he said. 'I don't take the Academies seriously so I'm not going to take the Logies seriously.'

Back in the United States, his co-star, Linda Kozlowski, had been keeping a low profile, even though 'Crocodile' Dundee had given her career a huge and largely unexpected boost. Suddenly she was in demand. 'It's a dream come true,' she said. 'It's amazing. 'Crocodile' Dundee is really going through the roof and overnight the phone is ringing off the hook. The difficult part now is being careful about what I do next.'

But what she, and Hogan, would do next was almost inevitable. 'Crocodile' Dundee had been running for a year in Australia. In the United States close to 50 million had seen it, making Hogan a wealthy man. By the middle of 1987 he had made an estimated $15 million from his little fable. He could have made more by licensing 'Crocodile' Dundee products, but rejected the idea on the grounds that these would have to include knives. He didn't like the idea of children brandishing such weapons, even if they were only plastic toys.

There had to be a sequel. Originally Hogan was not keen on the idea, but as he saw the queues form outside cinemas and listened to the pleas of movie executives, he reckoned the character could go one more round. In collaboration with his son, Brett, he wrote a script in which Dundee is again in both the United States and Kakadu National Park. Linda Kozlowski and John Meillon were signed. As well as being producer, John Cor-

nell was appointed director, replacing Peter Faiman, who had a prior commitment to produce the opening extravaganza for the 1988 Australian Bicentennial.

To ensure that it would be the last movie featuring Mick Dundee, no matter who got on their knees and pleaded for more, he has called it *'Crocodile' Dundee II – Finish*.

Hogan will go on to make other movies but has no intention of busting a gut in the process. He will not do them for the money, but for the fun. His family is well provided for, he is not hungry for more. His lifestyle, lying beside a swimming pool, enjoying a few cans of Foster's with his mates, does not require the cashflow of an oil sheik. He is satisfied.

'I've got more money than I can spend. If you're not happy with that, a hand should reach down out of the clouds, give you a slap and say, "What do you want, you pig?" '

Suave, sophisticated, debonair . . . he's certainly come a long way from Lightning Ridge.

Acknowledgements

Many people have helped in the preparation of this book. I would like to thank Michael Willesee, Jimmy Fishburn, John Brown (Australian Minister for Tourism), John Meillon, Dulcie Boling (Chairman and Chief Executive, Southdown Press, Melbourne), John Hall (executive editor, Southdown Press, Melbourne), Frank Crook, Lurline Campbell (head librarian, News Ltd, Sydney), Sally MacMillan, Phillip Mason (Australian *Playboy*), Paul Ormonde (Carlton and United Breweries, Melbourne) and my colleagues in newspapers and magazines too numerous to mention. A special thanks to Craig Norris (product manager, Sony, Australia, Pty Ltd) for the generous loan of the Sony Model 10 word processor without which this book would never have been written. The Model 10 is highly recommended. And finally I cannot thank Marie Ussher enough, for it was she who cracked the gentle whip that kept me working to a tight deadline and contributed much to this book.

J.O.

Picture Acknowledgements

The author and publishers wish to extend their thanks to the following for providing pictures: Channel 9, Sydney, for those on pages 13, 18, 21, 23, 27, 28, 33, 37, 41, 42, 52, 53, 64, 79, 98, 99, 101-16, 118-22, 124-6, 147; Mike Nelson, Sydney, for those on 67 and 134-5; News Ltd of Australia for those on 72, 75 (Paul Johns), 89, 96, 128, 129 (Bob Martin), 137, 178; Scope Features, London (P. Carrette) for that on 176; Southdown Press, Australia, for those on 2, 6, 9, 10, 46, 51, 54, 57, 58, 61, 62, 66, 71, 78, 87, 90, 92, 117, 123, 130 and 159.

Bibliography

Adam-Smith, Patsy, *The Anzacs* (Thomas Nelson, 1985).

Baker, Sidney J., *The Australian Language* (Currawong Press, 1945).

Birch, Alan and David S. Macmillan, *The Sydney Scene 1788–1960* (Hale and Iremonger, 1962).

Bridges, Nancye (with Frank Crook), *Curtain Call* (Cassell Australia, 1980).

Cribben, John, *The Making of 'Anzacs'* (William Collins, 1985).

Dunstan, Keith, *Wowsers* (Cassell Australia, 1968).

Hornadge, Bill, *The Australian Slanguage* (Methuen Australia, 1986).

Jarratt, Suzy, *Movie Horses Down Under* (Horse Talk Enterprises, 1985).

Lawrence, Neil and Steve Bunk, *The Stump-Jumpers* (Hale and Iremonger, 1985).

Parsons, Fred, *A Man Called Mo* (William Heinemann, 1973).

Ramsay, Jim, *Cop It Sweet* (Allegheney News Service, 1977).

Willey, Keith, *You Might as Well Laugh, Mate* (Macmillan, 1984).

Other references include *Daily Telegraph*, Sydney; *Sunday Telegraph*, Sydney; *Daily Mirror*, Sydney; *The Sun*, Sydney; *The Sun-Herald*, Sydney; *The Australian*, Sydney; *The Sydney Morning Herald*, Sydney; *The Sun*, Brisbane; *Courier-Mail*, Brisbane; *The Herald*, Melbourne; *Northern Territory News*, Darwin; *The Times on Sunday* (formerly *The National Times*), Australia; *TV Week*, Australia; *New Idea*, Australia; *The Bulletin*, Australia; *Woman's Day*, Australia; *Cinema Papers*, Australia; *The Times*, London; *Los Angeles Times*, Los Angeles; *New York Times*, New York; *Washington Post*, Washington; *USA Today*, United States; *People*, United States; *US*, United States; *Newsweek*.